The Biggest City in America

Ohio History and Culture

Ohio History and Culture

The Biggest City in America

A Fifties Boyhood in Ohio

Richard B. Schwartz

 The University of Akron Press

All inquiries and permissions requests should be addressed to the
publisher, The University of Akron Press, Akron, OH 44325-1703

Manufactured in the United States of America

First Edition 1999
04 03 02 01 00 99   5 4 3 2 1

The paper used in this publication meets the minimum requirements of
American National Standard for Information Sciences—Permanence of Paper
for Printed Library Materials, ANSI z39.48-1984.*

Library of Congress Cataloging-in-Publication Data
Schwartz, Richard B.
    The biggest city in America : a fifties boyhood in Ohio /
Richard B. Schwartz.
        p.   cm. — (Ohio history and culture)
    ISBN 1-884836-49-6 (cloth : alk. paper).
    ISBN 1-884836-50-x (pbk. : alk. paper)
        1. Norwood Region (Ohio)—Social life and customs—
20th century.   2. Schwartz, Richard B.—Childhood and youth.
3. Norwood Region (Ohio) Biography.   4. Nineteen fifties.
I. Title.   II. Series.
F499.N8S39   1999
977.1'77—dc21   99-31367
                                                        CIP

For Franny Lang, Cincinnatian, with
my thanks for his wonderful daughter

Also by Richard B. Schwartz

Samuel Johnson and the New Science

Samuel Johnson and the Problem of Evil

Boswell's Johnson: A Preface to the LIFE

Daily Life in Johnson's London

After the Death of Literature

Frozen Stare (novel)

ed. *The Plays of Arthur Murphy*, 4 vols.

ed. *Theory and Tradition in Eighteenth-Century Studies*

Contents

Illustrations

Preface

The following memoir-stories are a series of reminiscences of my life in the 1950s in and around Norwood, Ohio. The city holds some inherent interest, at least to those of us who lived there, and I have tried to note items of such interest in the course of the stories. The principal purpose of the collection, however, is to combine memoir and reminiscence with narrative. I wanted to commit to writing the accounts that I have heretofore given in fragmentary, oral form, so that friends, family, and interested readers might find some harmless amusement in my personal recollections of a particular time in our national life.

Jeffrey Hart and other admirers of the 1950s have commented on the spectrum of experience which that period encompassed, a period, Hart notes, whose conception of beauty was so broad and generous as to include such widely divergent people and personalities as Brigitte Bardot and Audrey Hepburn. The 1950s are sometimes thought of as a time of relative peace within the bloody twentieth century (though the first third of the decade included the Korean "Conflict"), a time in which cultural affairs could attain in the national consciousness a position of prominence that is often reserved for war, though now it is being said the Cold War (an ongoing part of the period) was still a war and deserves its own monument in the nation's capital.

There is little in the pages that follow that concerns either the Korean or Cold Wars, though I remember fallout shelters and the radioactivity logo painted on the sides of water barrels gathering dust beneath grammar school stairwells. I am more interested in questions of religion, questions of relationships, questions of material culture, and questions of human development. These matters come together in fascinating ways in the 1950s, and their intersections are, I hope, of interest to others as well as to me.

Those intersections are seldom tidy and not infrequently awkward, though they are often the source of some humor. I find the 1950s a period of contradictions as well as comprehensiveness, of constraint as well as freedom, of release as well as conformity, of silence as well as new expression. Most of all, I find the 1950s distant. Its furniture continues to find a buoyant market in the shops of Melrose Avenue in Los Angeles, and its now-comic earnestness finds expression in such films as *A Christmas Story,* the account of a young boy's overweening desire for a Red Ryder BB gun and the disasters which accompany its acquisition.

To me these artifacts and events sometimes seem as distant as Upper Paleolithic cave paintings, despite the fact that I lived with them for a decade of my life, the pivotal developmental decade of adolescence. That distance is, in part, the story here, and the unwritten subtext concerns the nature of our own times, a story of what we can now take for granted and what we cannot.

I have not attempted any grand synoptic treatment of the period, and I do not pretend to believe that the experiences of a young boy in a small town in southern Ohio are representative of anything in particular. I do believe, however, that we aspire to live our lives as a continuous, rounded story with a somewhat orderly plot and a largely happy ending. What we often find instead are a series of disjunct and sometimes suspiciously connected scenes whose relative importance rises and falls with experience and whose moments appear, by turns, epiphanic or empty, Wordsworthian spots of time or awkward embarrassments. The fifties had more than their share of the two in combination, and I have attempted to trace a number of scenes from my own life in the hope that they might be of amusement and interest.

I believe in the importance of memory. I believe that we should remind ourselves of evil as well as good. Forgiving and forgetting are too often combined. We have abandoned some of the values of the fifties and embraced the shabby, just as we have minimized some of the period's wrongs by labeling them quaint and distancing them in time. What follows is neither a series of sermons nor a succession of tirades, but a set of honest recollections. In some ways, we were far freer then; in some ways, far less so. Unless we remember both tendencies of that period, we face greater difficulties in understanding and shaping the present.

The stories are arranged in approximate chronological order. I say *approximate* since experiences and events from other years are referred to in the course of individual stories. My purpose was to cover the decade and the events of my own life within it, without sacrificing a sense of the larger arc of my experience and the larger pattern of events in the world beyond my own.

With one exception, the stories present generalized accounts followed by specific incidents, my intent being to anchor the subject in both cultural detail and personal reminiscence. Despite their autobiographical thrust, I see the stories as consisting principally of observation and commentary and secondarily of personal narrative. The details are all faithful to my sense of the experiences described, and the great majority are literally true in each detail. Rare changes have been made in order to eliminate trivia and sharpen the focus. The stories (like all stories) have been shaped to accommodate the reader, but I have done so with a watchful eye on the original realities. I have changed most of the names of the people involved, but kept the actual names of a few individuals I particularly admired. Many of the others have been afforded a degree of protection they did not always deserve.

My personal heritage is German-Catholic, with a healthy portion of Irish and English blood. The family name was actually von Schwartz, hinting at some degree of status that seems hardly commensurate with my southern Ohio/northern Kentucky background. My maternal grandmother, however, was a Lowenstein (remember the little Lowenstein girl in *Schindler's List?*), so that I carry sufficient Jewish blood to have qualified myself for extermination at the hands of the Third Reich. My grandmother was a marvelous person, and, without entangling myself in the nature/nurture dispute, I believe that some elements of the stories that

follow—particularly their interest in the curiosities of human behavior—might somehow be traceable to that part of my family. In
short, these are German, Irish, English, Jewish stories, set in the
very middle of an America that has passed but whose memories
may be both amusing and in some way instructive for our own
time.

There are also pictures, each of them taken recently. Their purpose is twofold: to anchor the narrative and to point up the fact
that less has changed than one might at first think. The death of
industry here means the preservation of history. Lacking adequate
capital, developers permit old buildings to stand, unimproved but
untouched. Lacking an adequate tax base, the community relies on
fading facilities. Everything has changed, but everything, more or
less, is still there. Overgrown foliage covers chipped paint, but the
structures endure. The people who are left can still visit them.

The Biggest City in America

Elmwood

Golf Manor

Silverton

Swifton Shopping Center

Cincinnati Gardens

Losantiville Country Club

Fenwick Park

Bond Hill School

Bingo Hall

St. Agnes Church & School

Saints Peter & Paul School

Columbia

Holy Trinity Church

I-75

I-71

Saint Bernard

Norwood

Norwood Municipal Building

Norwood YMCA

Dorl Field

Pike-Montgomery Road

Fairfax

Cincinnati

Purcell High School

I-71

Ohio River

Hamilton County Courthouse

St. Louis's Church

KENTUCKY

N

0   1   2
KILOMETERS

0   1   2
MILES

Hamilton County

City Street/County Road

Major Road

City Boundary

State Boundary

Source Data:
U.S.G.S. 7.5 Minute Series Quadrangle Maps
U.S. Census Bureau TIGER Line Data

Produced by:
The Geographic Resources Center
Department of Geography
University of Missouri- Columbia.

1998

Sentimental Journey: A Troubled Dream

As God is my judge, my girlfriend's grandmother told me there was no reason to live anywhere in the world but Norwood, Ohio. When I politely asked why, she said that it was obvious—because Norwood had so many advantages. When I (still politely) asked for an example, she searched her memory for about ten or fifteen seconds and finally came up with what she considered to be a very good one: unlike a number of lesser cities, Norwood had always had, and doubtless always would have, free garbage pickup. Unlike the benighted northwest suburbs where one was forced to hire a company such as Chris Rumpke's for trash removal, the progressive city of Norwood provided the service without any charge. Her judgment of Norwood's avant-gardist position was prophetic, since Rumpke's trucks and industrial Dempster Dumpsters are still very much in evidence forty years later in those "other" suburbs.

Karen's grandmother was one of my special memories of the "Gem of the Highlands" (as the city's website describes it). Among other things, she could always be counted on to provide humor while she was busily instilling terror. For example, once every six months or so on a gray Sunday morning she would announce to her husband ("Pa") that she wanted to drive the family home from church. The resulting ride was something that would have given Mack Sennett a spastic colon: oncoming drivers rolling their eyes in abject fear and shaking their fists in slow-boiling rage; children and small animals leaping for the safety of the nearest tree or side-walk; Grandma's passengers covering their eyes like See-No-Evil; and Pa squirming quietly, trying to close his eyes without Grand-ma noticing, and thrusting out his chin and Adam's apple as if he were trying to work his head back inside his starched collar like a cartoon ostrich. At least I got to hold their granddaughter's white-knuckled hand for the mile and a half between St. Matthew's Church and their home adjoining Thiemann's Cleaners.

She was a strong woman, but increasingly dotty. Her measure of civic responsibility was the regular cutting of grass, an obliga-tion discharged by her grandson, Karen's brother John. By her measure, the grass required cutting whenever one of the neighbors cut his. Thus, John was directed to repeat the process whenever she heard the sound of a nearby mower in operation. Sometimes he was forced to cut the grass three times in a single week. The ac-tual length of the grass was considered irrelevant. No self-respect-ing resident of Norwood would want his or her grass to be longer than the neighbors', regardless of the grass's actual height, so that the grandson's protestations were always overruled.

So this was a Norwood booster of the most devoted variety. To the uninitiated out there, Norwood, Ohio, happens to be the sometime home of Allis-Chalmers tractors, a Fisher Body plant (birthing center for the Chevrolet Camaro), Eagle-Pitcher, Amer-ican Laundry, U.S. Playing Card, and a succession of automobile dealerships, preeminently, Schmidlapp Oldsmobile; the seat of no less than two White Castle restaurants and the former residence of George Chakiris, with an occasional visit from Roy Rogers (known in those days as Leonard Slye), and—from neighboring Evanston—Doris Day (née Kappelhoff). Its Little League giants included a team by the name of Just Dickman's. Sponsored by Dickman's Cafe (kitty-corner from the U.S. Playing Card plant on the south), its owner was asked what name he wanted on the team's uniforms. When he replied, "Just Dickman's," the man from the league took him literally.

Norwood is nothing less than the largest city in the United States (without a hospital or cemetery within the city limits). You can still count on every resident's telling you that. You can also count on the fact that they will not pause for a moment and ask themselves, "Who, in the entire Milky Way galaxy, could possibly be expected to care?" because they are still true believers. They will also tell you that it used to be an even better place to live (possible translation: back when the race restrictions on the real estate deeds were still strictly enforced). They will tell you that it is progressive (translation: the main drag has been torn up and replaced by a succession of pink and lavender strip malls). They will tell you that it is quiet and peaceful (translation: all the major industries died out or left). And they will tell you that it is a place with true family values (translation: the billiard hall closed when they broke up Montgomery Road, and they stopped selling dirty pictures in the Point Smoke Shop when Hugh Hefner came along and made that sort of thing legal).

Back when I was seeing Grandma and Pa's granddaughter, the town had a few other claims to fame. For fifty cents, you could take a cab ride to any location within the city limits—the hell with the bus and the sweaty passengers lugging their shopping bags aboard. (At least a dozen times, my grandmother told me this true story: a notoriously rude Cincinnati bus driver was finally disciplined for insulting one of his passengers. A heavy, middle-aged woman got on with a large bag of oranges that, unfortunately, promptly proceeded to break. As she bent over to retrieve the oranges which, by then, were rolling all over the floor of the bus, she broke wind audibly. The driver responded in an equally audible stage whisper, "That's the way, lady. If you can't catch 'em, shoot 'em.") When we wanted to go to the movies at the Ohio, the Plaza, or the Norwood (19¢, 35¢, and 50¢ respectively), or go to Waterworks or Victory for a swim, we got five kids together who could each come up with a spare dime and rode in style.

Norwood was the home of the first Twin Drive-In. (When you drove in, they asked you "Which side?") Norwood was the home of the Big Mama restaurant, early and very short-lived competition for Dave Frisch's Big Boy, which started out on the other side of town but spread our way fast. High school students laughed

The Norwood Municipal Building

The U.S. Playing Card plant, with Bicycle logo visible

Doris Day's childhood home, now overgrown

Dickman's Cafe

hysterically when the Big Mama waitresses took orders, writing down "1 BM"or "2 BMs." Norwood was the home of the Eat 'n' Park restaurant (quickly retitled the Eat 'n' Puke), which did great business on the one night a week that the Big Boy across the street was closed. Norwood was also the home of a chain of dairy stores that were able to offer discount prices because the milk they sold had substandard butterfat content.

In earlier times, Norwood was the home of a group of Native Americans called the Mound Builders. I saw one of their mounds once. It was shaped like a long, twisty snake. It was up by the north Norwood public tennis court, a couple of blocks east of Montgomery Drugs, a store specializing in trusses, canes, vaporizers, lemon phosphates, and soups and chili displayed in cans which were opened, emptied into a polished, stainless steel bowl that plugged into the wall, and heated before your very eyes. Now the serpent mound is surrounded by apartment buildings and crisscrossed with power lines. The drugstore is a bar.

We moved to Norwood for one irrefutable reason: its police and fire departments required their members to live within the limits of the city, and captive buyers made for stable property values. With memories of the depression never too far away, stable property values were something we definitely wanted. The town was surrounded on all sides by Cincinnati and formed part of that extended area that local car dealers and weathermen termed the tri-state.

The lines of demarcation between the two cities were drawn clearly. Norwood had a mayoral (as opposed to Cincinnati's council-manager) system of government. It also had a populace that was, save for one family, exclusively white. A significant portion of Cincinnati's residents came to Norwood to work in its industries, returning to their homes beneath the Ohio River on weekends.

With these well-traveled roads from Appalachia, local prejudices developed along geographical rather than racial lines, the racial lines being subsequently drawn by the white poor who feared black incursions in the industrial economy. Thus, the second largest social, racial, or ethnic group after "us" were the "hillbillies," and "hillbilly" was a common adjective, connoting an absence of style or savvy. Even today, a card hand containing three pairs is referred to as a "Norwood," suggesting the existence of three families living under the same roof. The city is also occasionally termed "Noritucky."

In the 1950s, you had to go downtown in Cincinnati to find the chili parlors, to shop at Shillito's, Pogue's, and McAlpin's, or to dine at one of the four-star restaurants (Maisonette, Pigalle's, and the Gourmet Room, the last of which revolved), and there were still some memories of the old *Island Queen*, a paddlewheeler which transported people from the downtown riverbank up the Ohio to Coney Island (Cincinnati's version). The *Queen* burned, and Coney Island was later replaced by King's Island, out on interstate 71, the road to Columbus. They kept something called Riverbend on the old Coney site. You can go there in the summer and hear singers like Julio Iglesias or Robert Goulet.

I learned about some of the recent changes when I returned recently for my wife's high school reunion. It was held right in Norwood, at the new Quality Courts. One of my brothers-in-law couldn't say enough about the place. He and his family go there for holiday dinners, because of the choice of four entrées and the all-you-can-eat dessert parfaits. I had some time free on the second day, and in the early evening I walked up Montgomery to the old neighborhood, saw the place where I used to get my hair cut, had a couple of bottles of Wiedemann's beer at the bar near the serpent mound, passed the building where my friend Larry's mother worked taking telephone orders for Sears, and tried to find the site of an old supper club that featured a live orchestra which broke into song ("We know where you'r-r-re go-o-oing!") every time somebody got up to go to the toilet.

At the top of the hill, before the road twisted and trailed off into Pleasant Ridge, sat the remains of our old church, Saints Peter and Paul's. Now they call it Holy Trinity, because attendance fell off and they had to close down the other two churches in Norwood (St. Matthew's and St. Elizabeth's) and consolidate the remaining faithful into a single parish. The new name still seems a

The pike, facing north

Saints Peter and Paul's School

Holy Trinity Church, formerly Saints Peter and Paul's, with statues of each remaining on either side of the door

bit contrived, since Peter and Paul were carved into the stone adjoining the front door of the church and they're still standing
there.

A block down the street was what was left of the old grammar
school. Morning mass meant a march up the hill, in ranks. Upon
entering the church, the St. Pete's students were expected to genu-
flect together and say, aloud, "Blessed be Jesus in the most Holy
Sacrifice of the Altar." I think that's what we were supposed to say.
Maybe it was "*and* the most Holy Sacrifice." I was never really
sure. If I could have called up a replay, it wouldn't have helped,
since generations of kids had reduced the prayer to a long and
largely unintelligible mumble long before I arrived at the school.

I did remember my experiences as a fourth and fifth grader
walking back from the church. On rainy days in that corner of the
soggy Ohio Valley, we were advised to carry umbrellas or wear yellow rubber raincoats, though many couldn't afford them. Whenever we passed under wet tree limbs, the handles of the boys' umbrellas went up, and the leaf-drenched limbs were jerked to soak
the hatless little girls. The boy victims fared even worse, with handles slipped carefully between their marching legs, followed by a
quick groin-grabbing pull.

The pastor was an old Dutchman (translation: German) named
Bremmer who talked incessantly about two things: giving money
and making money. When he wasn't reciting a list of upkeep costs
or the size of the parish's subsidy to the school, he was urging us to
support local politicians and judges committed to upholding the
solemn distinction between illegal "gambling" and legal bingo.
One of the principal supporters of this distinction was a Jewish
judge named Benjamin Schwartz. When Father Bremmer met my
father Jack, an Episcopalian, he mistook him for the judge and
shook his hand and arm harder than Beowulf did Grendel's.

Father Bremmer also reminded us of our responsibility to participate in the auxiliary enterprises which he had worked so hard
to establish. We scraped and scratched for years in hopes of the
parish's eventually building a school gym, spending hot August
days manning the booths at the annual church festival and clear-

ing splintery picnic tables at the Friday night fish fries. Our per-
petual dream was a hardwood basketball court (not some crappy
linoleum job like the one they had at Allison Street School, but a
real Seal-O-Sand special). An adjoining pool would have been
nice, but we knew Bremmer and decided it was pointless to push
our luck. The gym was never built, but the bingo hall adjoining
the gym's proposed site was absolutely state-of-the-art, with at
least a dozen beer taps, a PA system that would have made Metal-
lica proud, and off-street, paved parking for 125 cars and a full row
of buses.

Father Bremmer's assistant (they didn't have associate pastors
in those days) was an angry middle-aged alcoholic named Lock.
In addition to their disagreements on nearly every other subject,
he and the pastor had different preferences for altar wine. Father
Bremmer wanted sweet, Father Lock wanted dry, and neither was
very happy if a rookie server got confused and mixed them up. It
was Father Lock's job to finish training the servers after Sister
Stephen got finished with them, and it was not a job that he rel-
ished. His favorite expression was, "Listen to me now, because I'm
only going to tell you this once. . . ." His proudest moment was
when he announced his solution to the age-old problem of the
single server. How does a right-handed, awkward fourth grader
pour both the wine and the water into the chalice with equal
grace? Easy (but he only told us once): after you pour the wine
with your right hand, you extend the little finger of your left. You
slip the wine cruet handle over your little finger and inconspicu-
ously transfer the water cruet to your right hand. Then you could
pour away with ease.

There were a couple things he didn't teach us—like how to
light the tall altar candles after somebody had smushed down the
wicks with the extinguisher or how to avoid the temptation to
sample the remains of the pints of Four Roses and Old Grand
Dad which the men from the choir thought they had successfully
hidden in the backs of their lockers.

Father Bremmer left the bulk of the training responsibilities to
Lock, with one exception—the disposal of the incense briquet.

Whenever there were ceremonies calling for incense, the servers were required to get the censer briquet going just before the ceremonies began. Bremmer loved smoke and liked to dig around on an already hot briquet before covering it with incense. After the ceremony had ended, he personally supervised the dumping of the smoldering remains into a large flower pot just outside the sacristy door. He was concerned that neither the church nor the surrounding bushes be set ablaze, and he frequently required the servers to douse the remains with water before completing their other tasks.

While Father Bremmer liked to work the censer, filling the church towers with sweet-smelling smoke, Lock liked to spray the parishioners with holy water. He would dip the perforated tube deep into the plated bucket and then snap his wrist with abandon, aiming especially for eyes, glasses, newly coiffed hair, and the faces of bored children. This was apparent to the servers, but not to the parishioners. No one ever seemed to realize that he took such pride in his marksmanship. They always fell to their knees, making the sign of the cross as they uttered silent prayers.

An English friend of ours divides contemporary Catholic churches into two opposing categories: "happy-clappy" or "smells-and-bells." St. Pete's was definitely smells-and-bells; there was virtually no clappy and even less happy.

When I saw it, the church looked pretty much the same as it always had. Behind the altar was a huge mural consisting of the principal saints, wearing their assigned crowns as they participated in a heavenly procession. The crowns were of different sizes and shapes, and it was clear that some were top-of-the-line while others were more standard production items. Sister Geraldine used to explain both the differences and the reasons for the differences in a set speech that ran for an hour and fifteen minutes. I've forgotten most of it, but some of the memories came back when I saw the pieces of palm projecting from the crowns of Saints Felicitas and Perpetua.

The rear of the church was shut off by a wall of wood and glass, to keep noisy children from interrupting the good father's sermons and to prevent the loss of heat or air conditioning when the outside entry doors swung open. The pastor's explanation of why you "didn't really hear mass" from the other side of the glass was a set speech that ran for thirty minutes. When Sister Stephen overheard one of my sixth-grade classmates suggesting that it was probably because they didn't take up the collection back there, he was given a stern reprimand and a check mark on the deportment side of his report card. He lucked out in saying it in front of Sister Stephen rather than in front of Geraldine. Gerry would have spread his knuckles over the top of the radiator and gone to work with the metal edge of her ruler.

She never got me, but she got my friend Larry. It was the middle of February, and he had been accused of melting a red crayon on the old silver-painted radiator. She learned about it from one of her snitches but waited to punish him until after he came in from recess, his hands well chilled from making snowballs. Before giving him a chance to answer the charges, she started in on his shivering, open palms with the business end of a yardstick, one that had a leather thong she always slipped over her wrist to strengthen her grip. She hit him eight times on each hand. She never broke the skin, but she left a couple of fine welts. Larry had trouble writing for four days.

I walked around to the back of the school. Across the crumbling asphalt, I could see the new bingo hall. There was still no gym beside it, just a single rusty backboard with a bent, netless rim. The schoolyard was dotted with dandelions and giant foxtail. It all looked smaller, as childhood scenes always do. To the left, I saw the corner where they set up the festival booths each August. Beyond it, the asphalt had crumbled and fallen toward Fenwick Avenue like a black, stony waterfall.

The ham booth was always situated in that corner, and it was always popular with the poor, who hoped for a weekend's worth of meat for a 25¢ ticket. The adjoining beer booth consistently drew the men. The kids hung out at the booth with the giant plush dolls, the boys doing their best to win a panda or a teddy bear, so they might promptly hand it over to a young girl who might respond with a kiss or a kind word.

I especially remembered the mouse roulette booth. It consisted of a giant, horizontal wheel with color-coded holes around the edge. Under each hole was a cup. The patrons put their money on one of the color panels on an oilcloth strip, thumb-tacked to the wooden counters, and waited as the wheel was spun. In the center was a mouse under a cup. As the wheel rotated and the cup was lifted, the mouse turned around, got his bearings, ran off to the edge of the wheel, and tried to escape down a colored hole. The color was announced, and the lucky winners were paid off. The mouse was retrieved, still in the new cup, taken back to the center of the wheel, upended, and covered. The former cup was put in place of the new one. This went on all day, for the whole weekend. Underneath the wheel was a cage with two or three reserve mice. They were occasionally rotated with the current one when he got too dizzy or tired to try to escape.

The festivals made a lot of money for Father Bremmer, but we always thought they were a little cheesy. He brought in circus acts for the little kids and raffled off stripped Plymouths or sets of gawdy rattan porch furniture to attract the attention of their parents. One year he brought in Clarabell the clown from the Howdy Doody show, the character who used to be played by Bob Keeshan, the guy who later played Captain Kangaroo. We all knew it wasn't the real Clarabell. It was obvious that you could have hidden anybody under all that makeup, and we knew that Bremmer would never have sprung for the first team. The only requirement was to be able to honk the horn on that box attached to his belt. There was also this guy dressed up like Buffalo Bob, but it wasn't really Bob Smith. They called him Buffalo Carl or something. They told us he was Buffalo Bob's brother.

My friend Larry liked the high-wire acts. They usually had women in scanty costumes who hung by their hair or their teeth and twirled above the parking lot. One year we went into the bingo hall to take a leak and walked down the hallway next to the beer taps. There was a room there in which Father Bremmer used to count the cash and store his files. The high-wire act was using it as a dressing room, and, when we walked past it, the door was slightly ajar. A guy was standing there in his underwear, and the girl was standing next to him, wearing some kind of shiny corset thing with a push-up bra. They were smoking and speaking a foreign language (Larry said it was Romanian, but I knew he was just guessing).

I turned and looked at the back of the school and noticed that the small windows of the doors on the ground level had been boarded up. In the front of the building, they had just pulled down the blinds, so I had figured that the school was only closed for the weekend. I walked closer, climbed the three steps up from the schoolyard, and tried the door. I didn't expect it to be unlocked and was surprised when it opened far enough to expose a heavy chain connecting the inside panic bars on either side.

With the door open, I could see the right corner of the old auditorium and part of the stage. At noon, the auditorium doubled as a cafeteria, and, on the mornings of holy days and first Fridays, they sold raspberry sweet rolls and cocoa to those who had fasted and taken communion. Show-offs prided themselves on the number of sweet rolls they ordered and ate. Some ate as many as six rolls and then tried to talk the wimps out of theirs. At lunch, the staff brought out steam tables and sold food to kids with enough money to buy their lunch rather than bring it.

They also used the auditorium for the annual visit of the Coca Cola distributor. He showed us a movie about how the company bottled Coke (down on Dana Avenue, just beyond the Norwood city line) and then gave everybody a free bottle to sample. It was also the place where they distributed saplings on Arbor Day and administered Salk polio vaccine. That was in the days before Sabin sugar cubes, when the vaccine had to be worked under the skin with the point of a long needle. Some of the younger kids panicked when they saw the needles and heard their screaming classmates. The nuns' solution, as God is my witness, was to put the head and shoulders of the fearful out the window and close the bottom frame on their upper arms. Then one of the nuns grabbed the right or left wrist and held the arm rigid while the doctor or nurse worked the needle and the kid sobbed and flailed.

We were tough fifth graders when the first vaccine arrived, refusing to let anyone think we were frightened, but the first and second graders were ready for triage. One of the kids restrained by a window sash went into convulsions, while a second jerked forward, hitting his forehead on the pane, nearly shattering it. The doctor jumped back, and the syringe fell out of the kid's arm. Gerry went outside, held his head and shoulders down, and told the doc to give him the needle again.

I was thinking about all that as I walked around to the door on the west side of the auditorium. It was the door the boys always used, because it was opposite their toilet, a noisy and smelly place that should have provided a temporary haven against the discipline of the nuns, but didn't. They walked in without warning, checking for any form of forbidden activity they could describe or imagine. There were no drugs then to speak of and little vandalism, so what it was they were really doing there we never learned. Maybe it was just the opportunity to deny us any sense of privacy or freedom from their constant stares.

Standing on the steps outside the door, I reached for the handle in what I knew was a pointless exercise. I slid my thumb over the lock release and pressed. I suppose I just wanted to feel the brass. I wanted to try to remember the moments—rushing in, late for class, or, on rare occasions, early—remembering to leave time for a trip to the drinking fountain, trying to store enough water to get me through a hot and humid Cincinnati afternoon.

At first there was resistance, but I pushed harder, and the bolt retracted. I pulled gently, and the door opened, the plywood behind the window making a slight scuffing sound as it cleared the steel jamb. I opened it farther and walked into the hallway. The tile was dusty, but free of the old smells: urine, disinfectant, the green sawdust the janitor threw on the floor when a kid puked, cooking grease, mildew.

I went into the toilet. By now it was nearly dark. I could see

The parish bingo hall, newly remodeled

The Salk vaccine windows

that most of the salvageable porcelain and copper had been removed. The room looked like the remains of an industrial facility that had failed to keep up and was eventually abandoned. There were some indelible rust stains on the floor and some old scratches on the green, enamel paint flaking from the walls. I crossed the hall and opened the door to the auditorium. It swung open easily.

The room was just as I remembered it, but smaller. The stage was still in place, though the faded, red velvet curtain was gone. The windows that held the polio vaccine recipients in place were all still there. There were even some stacked, steel foldup chairs in the east corner of the room, near the main exit doors. I walked to the front of the auditorium, went around the front of the stage and into the kitchen area. All of the ovens and sinks had been removed, but the central work table was still in place, bolted to the tile floor.

By now the room was almost completely dark, and I decided to walk up the steps to the main floor of the school. I knew that everything of value would be removed, but I wanted to see the wall that held the trough for the bank of drinking fountains. The nuns patrolled it carefully each morning, reminding any intended communicants that they shouldn't break their fast with a single sip of water. I wanted to see if the principal's office was still there. The shelves of Hummel figurines would all be gone, but the massive oak desk—a relic already in the fifties—might still be in place. While I was there, I could check on the wiring for the elaborate intercom system that she used to eavesdrop on classes as well as to make "Now hear this" announcements in one or more rooms simultaneously.

Sister Origen. Second only to Geraldine in her capacity for dispensing pain and instilling terror. She got me for nine long years. I arrived in fourth grade, but that was just the beginning. When we went to high school, the parish split the cost of diocesan school tuition with the parents. That meant that we had to return to the grammar school to receive our report cards. Father Bremmer distributed them in Origen's office. She beamed with pride at our success, taking a large share of the credit for our performance. She also stared daggers if our grades were low, Bremmer providing the narrow-eyed, narrow-lipped sermon on our representing a bad in-vestment for the parish as well as for our parents. Lifetimes of fail-ure were confidently predicted, Origen reinforcing the pastor's as-sessments with accounts of dark past histories.

The door had been removed from her office, and there was nothing left to remind me of her presence except for the bent, cor-roded wires protruding from the east wall. The table that had held her microphone and the bank of switches that had opened the channels to three floors of classrooms were all gone. I could hear her voice echoing in the back of my head. When I was in seventh grade, she guest-taught math. Whenever she screwed up a com-putation and we called it to her attention, she twisted up her face and gave us some bullshit like, "Almost caught you *that* time." I felt sorry for Sister Elizabeth. She had to stand by and act polite whenever Origen came into her room and took over her class. Sis-ter Elizabeth was one of the few nice ones. Smart, too. Origen was a crone. The queen of the crones. That's probably why they made her principal. She taught the rest of them.

The front door of the school, just opposite Origen's office, was bolted tight, so I returned by way of the south stairs, past the toi-let, where the fifth-grade girls huddled and passed around their menstruation textbook *(Starring You)*. One of the girls showed it to us once; it was lame—weird anatomical line drawings com-bined with pictures of girls in prom gowns.

When I got to the landing, one flight above the auditorium, I thought I heard something, something coming from the dark, a slight sound of movement, a hand along a rail or a padded shoe on a dusty tile floor. I turned and listened. Nothing. I took a step for-ward, still listening. Again there was nothing. One more step. Nothing. Everything was OK.

I looked toward the ceiling and saw a hole in the plaster that had been covered by some tape that had dried and loosened. The air from the other side was moving the ends of the tape against the side of the wall. I don't know what I expected—a nun with a trun-cheon coming after me? None of them went into security work when they left the order. A missed opportunity, perhaps. Most of them just retired, took up their real names (Joan, Mary Beth), and lived out their days.

The nuns who taught at St. Pete's also taught at Regina High, the all-girls school that sat on a rise just beyond the bingo hall. Years ago, it was torn down for apartments. The nuns always seemed closer to the Regina alumnae than to their students at St. Pete's. They had brutalized the Regina girls in subtler, more easily forgotten ways.

The rooms at Regina carried geographical names, some less than politically correct. The most distant was Jupiter, the most sunny California, the room without windows, Ethiopia. Even as a high school student, I wondered what drove people to give such names to rooms. Ethiopia was a particularly important room. That was the room to which the Regina girls were obliged to go on the nights of their junior and senior proms. In Ethiopia, the girls' prom dresses were inspected by the nuns, who had bolts of material at the ready. The slightest hint of décolletage brought the nuns' scissors to port arms. They then quickly fashioned drapes from the bolts of available material and required the girls to wear them.

They didn't have to worry about the girls' dates at that point, since they had required the girls to submit the names of their dates (and their dates' parishes) well in advance of the event, the purpose being to give them adequate time to verify the parish membership (and hence, the Catholicism) of the boys. Any attempts to date a non-Catholic, avoid the mandatory trip to Ethiopia, or discard the material covering the décolletage were seen as serious repudiations of proper authority and grounds for punishment of various kinds.

The dresses (with or without plunging necklines) were a welcome break from the school uniforms: white blouses covered by blue vests, designed to hide any hint of the feminine form, with blue skirts that quickly became shiny in the seat unless they were constantly drycleaned. When the nuns were not bracing (and, often, publicly humiliating) the girls for some petty infraction, they were passing them secret notes, suggesting to them that they should give prayerful thought to the possibility that they might have a vocation.

Their batting average in this area was poor, perhaps because sadism and invasion of privacy were not the activities with which most young girls hoped to occupy themselves in the years ahead. What I could never finally understand was how these women could turn civilian, recover their civilian names, and then attempt to strike up relationships with the women they had earlier mistreated.

The former nuns gave my grammar school classmates a wider berth, but there were still occasional overtures. How could these people, who had twisted our psyches, bent, folded, spindled, and mutilated our spirits, and treated our parents like ignorant, misbehaving children, suddenly try to pass for normal and expect us to respond to them in similar fashion?

As I stood in the gravel and broken asphalt of the parking lot, looking up at the apartment buildings, I thought of the many afternoons when we had driven from Purcell to Regina, parked along Quatman Avenue, waiting patiently for our girlfriends to appear, so that we could drive them home. We never went inside, because our presence brought stares from the nuns that could make a basilisk blink.

There was no reason to go inside now. They were all gone and with them their school, their convent, their shrines ("O Mary we crown thee with blossoms today / Queen of the an-gels, queen of the May"), the IHS rings that they used to strike our cheeks and eyes, the ruler edges that came down upon our knuckles, the notes they passed inviting our girlfriends to be brides of Jesus, and the host of techniques for instilling guilt, denying desire, and bending youthful imaginations to the iron will of the repressed fanatic. All that remains vital of their schools and their school grounds is the solid, low-slung facility that lay between St. Pete's and Regina, linking these two arms of Catholic education. The new bingo hall stood there, a squat but sturdy symbol of the parish's enduring values.

2

1950

The View from the Second Floor

During the war, my father was ineligible for military service because of a cyst on his spine, so he decided to do his part for the
country by joining the Federal Bureau of Investigation. The FBI
was then open only to CPAs and lawyers, my father qualifying as
one of the latter. His lack of a military uniform still drew suspicious stares on buses and trains, but he did his work, training at
Quantico and then serving in Omaha, Denver, Salt Lake City, and
other points west. For a time, he was assigned the task of busting
Mormons for practicing polygamy (I didn't hear the full stories
until I was older, but they were worth waiting for); at another
time, the bureau capitalized on his stenographic skills by assigning
him to attend communist meetings and taking notes on what tran-
spired there. He wasn't a big infiltrator of secret communist cells,
like Herb "I Led Three Lives" Philbrick. He just went to the public meetings.

He never had to tangle with headline criminals, though he did
know a man who was once shot by Machine Gun Kelly. This was
not a source of great pride to the man, since he had been shot in
the behind with a small caliber round, a fact he was reminded of at
regular intervals. When the war ended and, with it, my father's bureau tour, the family returned to Cincinnati, to an apartment in
Bond Hill.

Bond Hill adjoined Norwood, but it was culturally very distant.
In the first place, Bond Hill was predominantly Jewish. It featured

the California Deli which, curiously enough, specialized in New York food. The somewhat misleading name came from the fact that the deli was located on California Avenue, a street that also included St. Agnes's School, the site of my first initiation into the ways of the sisterhood.

For kindergarten, I had been sent to Bond Hill School, the Catholics not offering kindergarten in those days. This was a source of some trepidation to my parents, since public schools were always places of potential danger, at least in the Catholic consciousness. For the young, they offered (it was feared) unbridled violence and a lack of discipline; for the adolescent, (it was feared) they offered unbridled sex, or (far more dangerous) sex that was free of guilt. My experience there was actually very pleasant. The facilities were exceptional (they had the tax dollars and didn't need the bingo and bake sale income), and my kindergarten teacher was a living, breathing, published author, having written a very successful children's book entitled *Lazy Liza Lizard*.

Unfortunately, my time at Bond Hill School was brief, and I was off to St. Agnes's. There are three things that I remember vividly about that school. The first was Sister Noalita (instantly transmuted to "know-a-little," even on the lips of innocent first graders), who took it upon herself to teach me proper discipline. This she did with the skill of a hardened and suitably sadistic gunnery sergeant.

Noalita's specialty was unpredictable justice. As third graders, our notion of right and wrong, of reward and retribution, was simple. We agreed with Auda in *Lawrence of Arabia:* "He killed. He dies." If you hit, you got hit back. If you pinched, you got pinched back. If you butted up in line, you got sent to the end of the line. Noalita disagreed. Her responses were far less predictable:

"You hit him; you . . . stay in from the playground."

"You called her a name; you . . . do extra homework."

"You splashed his face with water from the drinking fountain; you . . . miss the field trip."

"You kept running around the schoolyard after the bell rang; you . . . apologize to me and then to the class."

Bond Hill School. The kindergarten room is on the first floor, at the far right.

St. Agnes's Church and School. Paper drives were held in the playground to the right rear of the church.

These unexpected responses, punctuated with noticeable pauses, gave rise to a belief in the existence of unwritten rules and the constantly reinforced suspicion that Noalita preferred summary forms of punishment to due process and transparency. In the years since, I have come to believe that there was some design lurking beneath the method. The absence of suitable equipment in the Catholic schools paralleled the absence of adequate instructional staff. Throughout my grammar school education, I sat in classes of at least fifty students. In Columbia, Missouri, that would now be grounds for a parental oath of the tennis court, but we sat there nonetheless. Sat quietly, that is, the iron discipline being a necessary corollary of the short staff. The sisterhood were taking their lessons from history. Their judicial system mirrored that of eighteenth-century England. Lacking a proper police force then, the authorities responded by making small infractions capital crimes. "You stole a handkerchief . . . you hang." The nuns inherited their system. "You were making faces at Roberta; you . . . go stand in the cloakroom with your face to the wall . . . for two days." (But how could you not love the notion of the "cloakroom," redolent of associations with musketeers' or Victorian gentlemen's garb?)

The second thing I remember about that school was the constant announcement of paper drives. St. Agnes's may have been short on bake sales and bingo, but it possessed more paper than a Government Printing Office warehouse or a Department of Energy recycling dumpster. Newspapers and the occasional magazine were stacked in humongous wooden bins and then packed into trailers for removal. These bins were near-permanent fixtures in the schoolyard at the rear of the building. I remember particularly the poorer kids from the neighborhood climbing into the bins, covering their heads with newspapers for the purpose of concealment and protection from the rain, and then proceeding to read the comic books that the more privileged kids had thrown away. Occasionally, there was an older boy in search of more adult fare, but such publications were rare (beyond the "foundation garment" ads in the Sears catalogue) and the pickings especially thin at St. Agnes's.

My principal memory was of Breithalle's, a grocery store adjoining the school on the west, which drew traffic from the surrounding houses and apartments as well as from St. Agnes's and Bond Hill School. Breithalle's had groceries, meats, and milk, but its staple was candy. Old man Breithalle ("Mr. Breithalle" always, to us) carried every variety of candy known to humankind, and he specialized in so-called penny candy, the unboxed, unwrapped, by-the-piece stuff which basically consisted of sugar and dye formed into a succession of interesting shapes and sizes.

The candy pipes were always big, as were the foamy candy ice cream cones. Licorice whips were also popular, both in black and red, for they served as weapons as well as food. We loved the miniature candy hats and the malted milk balls, the jellied swords and the jawbreakers. The all-time favorite, however, was a weird confection consisting of droplets of colored sugar affixed to long rolls of white paper. The droplets were aligned in rows, and the candy was purchased by the foot.

Money was tendered, and the paper was unrolled, exposing a foot or more of candy drops against a white background. The candy was consumed by holding the paper against your mouth and working your teeth around the sugar, being careful not to take in paper along with the sweet. This, of course, was impossible. You always got paper with the sweet, so that this candy was rich in fiber as well as sugar. It also brought with it the side effect of stained chins and lips.

My own favorite, along with the paper candy, was paraffin filled with sugary, colored liquid. This came in many forms, including the shape of miniature revolvers. You bit into the wax, got a sweet rush of liquid and flavoring, and then chewed the mess until it became dry and crumbly, at which point you spat it out for the edification of those around you. In the process, you were left with waxy bits of detritus between your teeth, the logical solution to this unpleasant dilemma being the consumption of a fresh wax candy.

Mr. Breithalle had tiny paper bags designed for small hands. He tried not to rush us as we pondered our selections, but sometimes his temper got the better of him, particularly if there were serious buyers in the store, checking out his steaks and roasts.

The California Deli was interesting as well, my favorite food there being the New York cheesecake. The deli was no more than three or four doors from the local Albers (Kroger's competition in those days), but it was always able to hold its own, Cincinnatians having become accustomed to the idea of four-stop or five-stop food shopping.

A few doors from Albers to the north were a drugstore, beauty parlor, and branch library. One day I returned some books to the library for an ailing neighbor and found a twenty-dollar bill on the sidewalk outside. Under Sister Noalita's tutelage, I immediately interpreted this as a divine gift for my practicing a corporal work of mercy. Just beyond these structures to the west was a country club called Maketewah, which formed a natural barrier between Bond Hill and the communities to the north. Maketewah was a gentile club in a Jewish neighborhood. It was an interesting place. Its fairways, for example, were interrupted by depressions that looked to us like giant chasms. These depressions were bridged by wooden structures. If you drove over the depressions, you were fine, but if you shanked your drive or dribbled it, you were ruined, for you had to climb down the side of the hill into the depression, hit the ball, and then climb back up again on the other side. Many, of course, failed to hit the ball up the other side on the first at- tempt and were trapped in the depression, hacking away, as their fellow golfers walked across the bridge, looking on with mock concern as they secretly delighted in their partner's dilemma.

When there were no golfers present, we liked to run across these bridges and listen to the sound of our feet echoing from the open space below. As we ran, we noticed the endless marks of the golfers' spikes. We worried about the erosion of the bridges' floor- ing and envisioned the plummeting of the unsuspecting players to the ground below.

Another interesting feature of the club was the fact that it offered skeet shooting. When the range was closed, we would sneak across the tees, fairways, and rough and into the shooting area, collecting unbroken clay pigeons which we would later use for dishes or targets. To the west of the range, just across the street from our apartment building, was a stand of trees ("woods" to us). In a ravine beneath the trees was a single, fallen tree which we termed the "lion tree," for reasons now forgotten, since it bore no resemblance to a lion. We assembled there, climbing and clambering and listening to the sound of drivers, of balls whistling through the air, of cheers and curses, and of distant shotguns.

My best friends were named Jim and Anne. We played together regularly, avoiding two of the other kids from the street, because the elder of the two always wanted to play doctor with her little brother, something we considered strange.

Her name was Cookie (real name, not a nickname), and her father owned a furniture store. Everyone in the family possessed a name that alliterated. He was Carl Cummings (of Cummings' Couches); she was Carol Cummings; the daughter was Cookie and the son Curtis. Cookie's principal interest in life was looking down Curtis's pants and announcing her discoveries there to anyone in the area who would listen. "Look at this, look at this," she would say, as we passed. We smiled politely, said hi, and kept moving.

Jim and Anne and I were more interested in trees and woods and clay pigeons than in the contents of Curtis's and Cookie's clothes. Jim lived two doors to the east, Anne three doors to the west. I envied the fact that Jim's mother was more daring than mine. She not only took him to see *Fantasia*, but she also somehow acquired a marquee still from the movie, which he prized. Whenever I was in his apartment, I asked to see the photograph, which his mother had had framed.

My mother had forbidden me to see *Fantasia* because she was concerned that it might frighten me. The picture of the demon on Bald Mountain suggested that this was not the standard Disney fare, but something odd, something adult. Mickey Mouse meets Stokowski. And sorcerers. And demons.

I was never in Anne's house. Her grandmother lived with them, and Anne told us that she was "crabby." Anne always met us or waited for us down at the lion tree.

Our apartment building was one of the most interesting places in which my family ever lived. Several of the residents were FBI agents, and several were radio and television people from the Cincinnati NBC affiliate. Word must have spread in the respective agencies and offices that 1421 Ryland Avenue was a good place to live. There were some other people in the building as well. Weird people. The weirdest was a woman who feared germs. She had two children, both boys, and neither was ever allowed to play outdoors, lest they somehow come in contact with the germs. When we did see them, they were so bundled up that they could hardly move.

One summer, she had to take them outside, probably to get shots for some imagined illness. It was a typical Cincinnati summer day, very hot and very humid. She appeared at the foot of the stairs behind the building and hurried her two boys to her car, which was parked in one of the double garages connected by a concrete apron behind the building. They were wearing winter coats, caps with earmuffs, and wool leggings. They looked like puffball robots or like Bib the Michelin man before the weight problem set in. Their mother nervously directed them as they attempted to walk, moving uneasily with their legs stiff and their arms extended from their sides.

Below us lived an FBI agent with an overactive libido. He was middle-aged and bald, and his wife's standard attire was a housedress and apron. They were both cheerful and friendly. Very friendly, in fact, for their bed rocked against the wall nearly every night with a force sufficient to wake all of those in adjoining apartments. My father teased him about it, and his standard response was, "I love my wife."

I didn't understand the bed rocking at the time, but I did later, and I was reminded of his comment when I was at an adolescent party with actual "party records," particularly the *Pardon My Blooper* records. One of the records was a recording of the sequence of the *You Bet Your Life* episode when Groucho Marx asked the contestant about the fact that he had more than a dozen children. The man replied, "I love my wife." Groucho quickly retorted, "I love my cigar, too, but I take it out every now and then," just as the microphone went dead.

The most curious resident of the building lived in the basement. He was the nephew of the landlord and must have fallen upon hard times. The owner constructed a "room" for him that consisted of a set of sheets stretched around four steel pillars, enclosing an area approximately ten feet by ten feet. Within that space was a bed, a dresser, and an overstuffed chair. The floor was cement, covered with two or three throw rugs, while the ceiling consisted of exposed wooden rafters and the base of the subfloor for the apartments above.

Just on the other side of the cloth room were the stationary tubs, the washers and dryers, the residents' lockers, and other common space. The occupant of the room was named Harold. He was seldom seen or heard, but he was there. Since there was no door through the stretched sheets, Harold had to get down on his hands and knees and slide under the bottom of one of the sheets. We always hoped that we would have the chance to see him do that, but we never did. Sometimes when Jim and Anne were over playing, we would go down to the basement, listen very carefully, and then lift the bottom of the sheet to see Harold's room. Fortunately, we were never caught. The act of lifting the sheets for a look at the room was something one was *dared* to do, though there was no reason to believe that Harold was dangerous. He simply lived in the basement of an apartment building in a room with cotton walls.

Our own apartment consisted of a kitchen with a breakfast nook, a large bedroom, a bathroom, a living room, and a playroom. The playroom contained all of my toys. It sat at the front of the building, just off of the main staircase for the apartments. There was, in fact, a window between my playroom and the stairway, with a simple latch. Sometimes I slipped through the window and into the hallway, knocking on our front door and surprising my mother. There were never any worries concerning security.

Breithalle's store

1421 Ryland Avenue. My playroom was at the center of the second floor above the entryway.

My playroom contained all of my treasures, in particular my collection of cap guns. These were all stored in an old white bathroom hamper (a wedding present mainstay then as now in Cincinnati). I had ninety-five cap guns, and their collective value on the antique market now would run into the thousands of dollars.

I played with guns endlessly, perhaps because of the fact that I grew up with them. As a bureau agent, my father had to go to the range periodically and test-fire those weapons that he could conceivably be called upon to use. Each evening, he brought home his own weapon, a .38 hammerless, cleared it, and set it on the top of the mantle. I was taught that guns were safe as long as they were empty. I was also taught that you never pointed a functioning gun at anyone unless you were prepared to kill that person. Thus, I became used to the presence of guns, played with toy guns, but never felt the need or interest to possess one as an adult. To me, a gun was a tool that you needed in certain lines of work.

Later, in the army, I fired pistols, carbines, rifles, machine guns, recoilless rifles, grenade launchers, mortars, and 105 mm. tank guns. The most lethal weapon in my house now is an O-Cel-O broom. Something happened in between my childhood and adulthood that permanently altered my interests, probably the discovery of women, always more dangerous than guns and far more interesting.

This discovery actually began in my apartment building on Ryland Avenue, not with Cookie Cummings, but with a redhaired resident from the third floor. She was an actress, or at least an aspiring actress, and people thought that she was very pretty. As a sixth grader, I might have registered a serious opinion, but that was several years off in the future. She also had friends who were pretty, and, on sunny days, they would sometimes take their blankets, walk across the street to Maketewah, and sunbathe on the side of the hill. Topless.

This was an occasion of great interest to the men in our apartment house, who talked about it endlessly, congregating in the front rooms of the building whenever the women were sunning themselves. Sometimes they used my playroom. I thought it was more interesting to watch them than to watch the women, since this was the only occasion on which the men demonstrated a deep interest and abiding curiosity in anything but work or sports.

This was also, I should hasten to add, before television, or at least the widespread availability of television. Aside from their weekly trips to the movies on Friday or Saturday evenings, this was the principal source of entertainment for most of the men in the building. It fascinated me. They would stare endlessly at the women, stretched out on old towels, talking and reading magazines. Their interest seemed to be in the size of the breasts they were observing, since there was a good bit of discussion on that topic. However, each of the mens' wives had larger breasts than those of the women on the blankets. Why were they opting for inferior specimens? There was also the curious fact that breasts (as body parts go) seemed so simple and uncomplicated. At the same time, they managed to be objects of intense scrutiny and subjects of judgments and discriminations more subtle than those of the scholastic philosophers. Unlike baseball games, hockey games, or small-screen television shows, they could also be observed without the presence of beer. This was fascinating.

One of the principal observers was a man named Bob Lynn. Bob was a broadcaster for NBC, moving from job to job during the time of our acquaintance. Starting as a television news and weather reporter, he was transferred eventually to the radio division, where he hosted *Moon River,* a late-night schmaltz show with dreamy music and greeting-card poetry. He finally plummeted to the role of announcer-interviewer for *Saturday Night Wrestling.*

I was impressed by the fact that Bob could adopt the language of each of these activities, moving from discussions of isobars and dew points to descriptions of figure-four grapevines, atomic drops, and Boston crabs. His bedroom closet contained a box of eight-by-ten-inch glossy photographs with preprinted signatures. He gave me one once and even mentioned my name on the air. He was my first introduction to show business.

His wife's name was Susan. Her principal occupations were to adore him and to send out copies of his photograph to inquiring fans. I spent a lot of time in their apartment, since they were the first people in the building to get a television set. On Saturday mornings, they let me come in and watch cartoons and serials while they slept.

Bob loved to talk. I think he wanted a child of his own, but, for some reason or other, he and Susan never had one. He liked to show me his things and explain them to me. He had a stack of old photographs, an assortment of 78rpm records, and a collection of antique weapons. His prize was a sword with a point that rose from four flat sides. When you looked at it from the point end, the shaft resembled an elongated cross. He told me that that sword was built in the "cross of Lorraine" style and that a cross of Lorraine sword inflicted a wound that would never heal. Watching his eyes as he described it, I felt as if I had been instantly transported to the crusades. Years later, I tried to find references to the cross of Lorraine in books of weaponry, but I could never find any.

Bob never forgot my birthday, but he remembered it in odd ways. One day I was in their apartment, and Susan was staring at me knowingly. He came out of the bedroom, wearing his pajama bottoms. His body was covered with sweat. I was struck by his bronze tan and wondered why he took the time to lay under heat lamps, timing his changes of position and being careful not to overexpose himself when, at that time in his career, he was broadcasting solely on the radio.

"How are you?" he asked.

"Fine," I said.

"You know what day this is, don't you?"

"Yes," I said.

"Your birthday," he answered, as Susan continued to watch and smile.

"Right," I said.

"We've got a little surprise for you," he said.

"Thanks," I said, not yet knowing what it was.

"It's in the bedroom."

"The bedroom?"

"Yes, go on in," he said.

This was not something I wanted to do, particularly with thoughts of the sheet-enclosed room in the basement or the rocking-bed bedroom in the apartment below us, but my curiosity was strong, and it was clear that Bob and Susan wanted me to go in and find my surprise.

I went in slowly and apprehensively, stopping at the door when I saw that their bed was unmade. They hadn't even bothered to straighten the sheets or reposition the blanket. In the film noir slatted light from the half-open venetian blinds, the bed looked as if it had never been made.

On the floor at the front of the bed was a set of weights. They were sitting out, right where Bob had left them after his morning workout. That explained the sweat. I looked around the room, my eyes searching for gift wrapping, bows, and ribbons, but there were none. I looked some more, finally going so far as to look under the bed, thinking that Bob might have hidden the present there, but there was nothing there either, except for some slippers, dust bunnies, and old crumpled Kleenex.

Bob called out from the living room. "Haven't you found it yet?"

"No," I answered.

"Well, keep looking," he said.

I checked the bookshelf next to his bed, but there was nothing there that resembled a present. I even looked in the closet that contained his box of publicity pictures, but there was nothing in it but a robe, Bob's suits, coats, slacks, and sweaters. I wondered where Susan's things must be and then remembered the cupboard in the hall. Perhaps the present was there. I started to walk toward it but remembered Bob's telling me that it was in the bedroom.

I thought about going through their sheets and blankets, but then thought better of it. Finally, I returned to the living room, empty-handed.

"Here," Bob said, "come on back. I don't see how you could have missed it."

He and Susan walked me down the hallway and into their bedroom. "It's right here," he said, reaching up in the air. On the top of one of the bedposts was a coonskin cap. Somehow I had looked right past it, expecting something wrapped. In the general disarray of the room, this was one more thing that was hanging on a knob or draped across the back of the chair, and I had completely overlooked it.

"Try it on," Bob said. Susan was standing behind him, her arms folded, waiting for my reaction. "It fits," he said, scrunching it tightly on my head after I had made the first, failed attempt.

"Thanks a lot," I said. "It's really nice." And it was. It was the real thing, not some imitation piece of junk you could pick up in a toy store. This was authentic. I guess Bob thought I had dreams of being Davy Crockett. It was the right part of the country. Davy had apparently fought with Mike Fink and the river pirates somewhere down on the Ohio. At least Disney thought he had, because they broadcast a story about it. Now there's a restaurant on the river called Mike Fink's.

It wasn't my line, however, and I never wore the cap. Part of the reason was that no one else had one, and, if I had worn it, I would probably have looked ridiculous (and been so labeled). The other reason was psychological, though I didn't think much about psychological things in those days. Every time I saw the cap, I thought about Bob and Susan's bedroom. It was someplace that I shouldn't have been, something that I shouldn't have seen, and the cap was forever associated with it.

It was the whole second-floor thing, and it didn't have anything to do with the loss of innocence. It had to do with showbiz people living at the margins, men with time on their hands, with a small apartment in a fringe neighborhood, filled with odd people whose lives were in a state of permanent drift. It was the sense that you were surrounded by abysses into which you could tumble at any moment. It was the feel of poverty and transience and uncertainty.

It was the feel of small spaces, small things, and imagined lives. A few months later, we moved. We were happy to leave, particularly since we were moving to Norwood. We were moving to our own house, a house where I would finally have my own bedroom. The coonskin cap went into a drawer. I can't remember what eventually happened to it.

3

1951

The Rich Are Different

The rich are different, as Hemingway said, because they have more money. But that doesn't tell half the story, even in Norwood, Ohio, where millionaires aren't exactly thick on the ground. Not that I had been exposed to all that many, my primary experience up until the age of eight having consisted of a single faux pas at a friend's house in Bond Hill. I knew he was certifiably rich because, in addition to a large house on a corner lot, which backed against the hurricane fence separating residential property from Maketewah Country Club, his parents owned something of even greater note: a Studebaker Land Cruiser. At that time, the Studebaker came in three models: the Champion, the Commander, and the Land Cruiser. We always bought Champions, so the opportunity to socialize with someone that far up the Studebaker food chain was duly noted by other friends and family.

The boy's name was David. I never met his father, who must have been working constantly to keep them in Land Cruisers, but I did meet his mother, the person before whom I embarrassed myself. It was no big deal, really. We were in David's kitchen, and I noticed that one of the water glasses on the counter had not been emptied. Actually, it wasn't a glass glass. It was one of those colored aluminum tumblers so much in fashion at the time. Among the so-called "Scrubbing Dutch" of Cincinnati, it was unthinkable to leave a glass on the sinkboard without emptying it, rinsing it, and turning it upside down to drain.

That, at any rate, would be the response of the lazy. The truly diligent would have emptied it, washed it, dried it, and put it in the cupboard, where it belonged. Since I was in someone else's house, however, I was also up against the "Never go into anyone else's cupboards" rule, so I emptied the glass of its remaining water, rinsed it, and set it on the sinkboard, upside down. It was the least I could do as a guest in David's house.

A few minutes later, when we were playing in another room, I heard footsteps. David's mother appeared at the door and asked the question, "Who threw out my Vichy water?" I am proud to say that I took immediate responsibility for this action and am able to report that David's mother did not make any heavy weather of it. I confessed that I thought it was regular water, and she told me that it was not important.

This was my first experience with people who didn't drink normal water. To this day, I cannot keep my hands off of an antique seltzer bottle or anything else aquatic that possesses a touch of the exotic. Water was a subject of serious concern to Cincinnatians. As grammar school students, we were taken to visit the city's water treatment facilities and were impressed with the care taken to insure a steady supply of potable water. We studied filtration and pumping systems and were warned constantly of the dangers of polluted water (principally the water of the Ohio River—remember your typhoid shots before entering). The water supply had also been a matter of significant controversy, since Cincinnati's vocal opposition to fluoridated water had made the national news. Some noted the existence of studies that purported to show that fluoridated water might be of some benefit to the young, but what of its effects on the elderly? What might happen to them? The application of fluoride to the city's water supply conjured up images of terrorist plots and Nazi research experiments, though the effort was finally labeled communist rather than fascist and the fluoridation plans promptly scuttled.

I didn't know about Vichy, France at the time that I pitched David's mother's water. Perhaps I should have been more suspicious of her. I did wonder at the time why she left her Vichy water in the kitchen when she was actually sitting in the living room. That was a most un-Cincinnati-like behavior. I decided that she had probably done so because of the fact that she was rich and, a priori, odd. I noted, for future reference, the likelihood that other curious behaviors might be associated with people of means, and I decided then and there to be on the lookout for them.

Later that year when we moved to Norwood, I found myself on a street with several rich people. The first was the favorite of the neighborhood kids, old Mr. Portz, who lived a half block away and gave away dimes as Halloween gifts. He was not only generous but also long-suffering. When we played touch football on the street next to his house, he never complained and never called the police. In fact, he never seemed to do anything. The only time we saw him was at his door, on Halloween, doling out the dimes. He was our notion of a perfect neighbor.

The other rich people on the street were our next-door neighbors, the Bensons. They had both a Pontiac and a Buick, a house with three bedrooms plus a usable attic, a side yard to the south with a garden, plus a side yard to the north with a swing set and a grill. The Bensons had three kids, the middle one (Larry) my age. I knew immediately that they were wealthy because of their house, their cars, and the quality of the electric trains in their attic playroom.

There was only one type of electric train that one would wish to have in 1951: a Lionel. ("That's real smoke a-puffin'; that's an engine you hear; I'm a Lionel [whoo, whoo] enginee-e-e-r!") Except that the smoke seldom puffed from the stacks of the locomotives on most peoples' trains; with the Bensons' the stacks actually worked. Every time. All the time. Moreover, they had the car that everyone had seen in pictures but never in nature: the one and only, certifiable, Lionel Milk Car.

The milk car assembly consisted of multiple pieces. First, there was a platform that was positioned on the side of the track. Then there was the milk car itself, with the pivoting milkman standing at the door of the car. Finally, there were the individual silver milk cans, which the milkman was to remove from the car and place on the platform.

This was a significant engineering feat, since the hands of the milkman and the milk cans were both magnetized. The idea was that the train would approach the platform, and the engineer (the kid operating the transformer—the Bensons had a transformer with two handles, one for each of their trains) would slow the train to a stop, such that the milk car would end up directly parallel to the milk car platform.

Meanwhile, the milk cans would already have been so positioned within the car that the milkman would be able to lift each of them (in a succession of fluid motions) and transfer them from the inside of the car to the outside platform. This required Normandy Invasion-level planning and positioning, but it always remained *possible*.

The reality was somewhat different. Since the milkman was attached to a mechanical pivot, his motions were less fluid than one might wish. Instead, they were more herky-jerky. As his body clicked from side to side and his hands and arms jerked from top to bottom, it was extremely difficult to achieve the results desired.

What usually happened was that it took several minutes of starting and stopping and backward and forward motion to position the milk car next to the platform. Then, when the milkman was activated, he began to jerk uncontrollably, pumping his arms up and down like a crazed referee signalling a dozen successful field goals.

At this point, the milk cans were either thrown sideways onto the platform, knocked over, or missed entirely. By the second or third attempt, the milkman's arms were simply jerking in space as the rest of the milk cans stood like silent sentinels, looking on.

This was a source of endless frustration. We spent hours positioning the milk cans, hoping for the proper result. Once in a great while, one of the cans was actually lifted and actually placed on the platform, though it was frequently knocked over in the succeeding attempt. However, we refused to be conquered, spending hours and days and weeks trying to get the milk car to respond to our wishes and cries. In all of that effort, I continued to be impressed by the simple fact of the milk car's existence and the fact that the Bensons possessed it as their very own.

They also owned an electric football game. These were far more common than the Lionel Milk Car, but nonetheless challenging. Electric football consisted of two teams positioned on a metal board painted to resemble a regulation football field. Each team was positioned for each play, and then a switch was turned on. The switch activated the board, which began to vibrate, the resulting vibrations causing the players to move about the field. Not all of the players moved in a forward direction. For the first several plays, we studied our teams, determining which players were the most reliable. The result most feared was the possibility that all of the players would move in different directions and the play simply fall apart, like the Monty Python soccer match between intellectuals who simply walk away from the center of the field, reading, pacing, and meditating.

This was a disaster if the defensive team moved forward, because significant losses of yardage could be incurred. Sometimes, however, both teams simply moved in odd directions, and the result was chaos and confusion. Electric football also offered the opportunity to both kick and pass, the game set including tiny cotton footballs. On rare occasions, passes were actually completed. The trick was to position the football in the passer's throwing cradle so that its flight could be controlled. Most of the time, it either stayed in the cradle or dribbled out onto the playing surface.

Our favorite pastime, however, involved a game called Star Reporter. Star Reporter was beautiful in its simplicity. Everyone began at a central point and drew assignment cards (cover the volcanic eruption in Hawaii; cover the zeppelin landing in Paris . . .). Then, turns were taken and dice rolled. First you had to go to the assignment site; then you returned to the home base to file your story.

This was a fantastic game. You got to travel all over the world and still return home in a matter of minutes. Unlike other games, this one offered us what we considered high drama without forcing us to concentrate too intently. Most of all, Star Reporter had an advantage over every other game of the roll-move-roll-move type. It was a colossal advantage, one so clever that we wondered why no one else had thought of it. It was an advantage that made Uncle Wiggly, Monopoly, Snakes 'n' Ladders, and the rest of them seem childish and simplistic.

With Star Reporter, you did not move tokens. You moved pins. In fact, you stuck the pins right into the board itself. This was just like in the real newsrooms and the real war rooms—little pins on a board representing the individuals or units within your organization. And when you moved, you could (and we did) stick your pin in every single space between your beginning point and your assignment site. The result was that the first two or three spaces in any direction from the start point were part of a gray, pulpy blob—the result of years of pinpricks.

Since we knew the number of spaces in this area, that did not prove to be a problem, though the realities always required an explanation for the hitherto uninitiated. There is something very real and very pleasant about pins stuck in a board, something we all felt. A sex-and-psych type from the Modern Language Association could analyze it endlessly. Star Reporter was the game for rainy days and for sunny days, for cold days as well as warm. We never tired of playing it.

On a few winter days, we went sled riding, either at the park or down Homer Hill, the kids' name for Homer Avenue, the long, angled street a few blocks to the east. In the summers, we played at the park, and, on rare occasions, we played in my basement.

The principal attraction of my basement was an orange basketball hoop fastened to the top of a door frame. Smaller than a regulation hoop, it was large enough to accommodate a junior-size basketball. When there was no one available for play, I played there alone, perfecting my shots. The low basement ceiling made that a significant challenge and gave new meaning to the notion of home court advantage. My childhood dream at the time was to make enough money to own a regulation-size basketball court. That would have been real wealth. A half court would have sufficed, so long as the goal, backboard, and net were all regulation. Instead, I played in my basement, endlessly practicing low-arc jump shots and set shots.

If the Bensons represented wealth, there were other neighbors who reminded us that many people were on stricter budgets. Norwood required all city employees to live within the city limits, so there was a high proportion of firemen and policemen in the neighborhood. With the adjoining industrial plants, there were also a number of mechanics, machinists, millwrights, lathe operators, and other craftsmen.

Directly across the street from the Bensons was a woman named Toennis who operated a barber shop/beauty parlor in her basement. This violated a number of codes, ordinances, and statutes, but Mrs. Toennis didn't seem to care. The fact that she gave free haircuts to some of the needy kids at the local school brought her significant brownie points and bargaining chips. Never a favorite with the other barbers and beauticians in the area, she could undercut their prices because she had so little overhead.

She still operated a professional shop, with the standard chair, blow dryer, sink, jar of blue liquid to fumigate the combs, tub of butch wax for those with flattops, and other appurtenances. Unlike her competitors, she also had Mickey and Tony.

Mickey was a mixed-breed canine, with a touch of poodle but a predominance of terrier. Tony was a blueblood, the parakeet's parakeet. If you believed Mrs. Toennis, Tony had the vocabulary of a twelve-year-old and the wiles of a Russian spy. Mickey was his constant victim.

Tony could mimic voices, particularly hers, and he would torment the dog in baroque ways whenever the mood struck him. His favorite trick was to light on the mantle and call out to the dog in a voice of mock love and concern, "Here Mickey. Here Mickey. Come on, Mickey. Nice dog. Nice Mickey. Come here boy. [the dog galloping toward the sound of his mistress' voice, putting on the brakes suddenly, stopping, looking around vainly,

5604 Fenwick Avenue, my home from 1950–60

My barbershop. The industrial strength fan is visible at the left of the garage door.

and finally hearing . . .] "Hel-l-l-o-o Mickey. He-l-l-l-o-o Mickey. Stupid Mickey. Stupid Mickey. Dumb dog!"

All the while Mrs. Toennis clipped and snipped, there were Tony and Mickey stories. One day I decided to both satisfy my curiosity and, potentially, call her bluff. I told her I'd love to see Tony in action. I had already seen Mickey, since he had the run of the house, the basement salon functioning (according to Mrs. Toennis) as a sort of sanctuary to which he might go to escape the cruelties and indignities inflicted by Tony.

Tony had the run (or the flight paths) of the main floor only, and it was somewhat disquieting to have him fly around your head. I quickly discovered that Mrs. Toennis's head and shoulders were among his favorite landing zones and worried that he might seek me out next. One Cincinnatism in which I had been well schooled was the notion that no one should permit a bird to fly freely through the house, the Scrubbing Dutch fearing the bird droppings as well as the disorder. This was related to the fear of having bats fly into your hair. In Cincinnati, presumably, the bats' sonar was inoperable, so that they could not help but land in your hair ("tangled" there—a favorite fantasy), bite you, give you rabies, and generally serve to spoil your entire day.

Tony was far too proud to be held to such plebeian rules as restrictions on air space. Boundaries were for dogs and lesser mammals such as humans, not for a relative of the dinosaurs. Mrs. Toennis happily agreed to take me upstairs to see the master at work. As she opened the door from the basement, I could hear the flapping of wings. This was wrong, all wrong. It reminded me of birds flying into schools and churches. They had no business there. Their presence was an accident bordering on sacrilege.

Tony disagreed and landed on Mrs. Toennis. He said nothing. This concerned me as well. What if her stories were all figments and phantasms? What if she was delusional? What sort of gothic nightmare was I entering?

Mickey was between our legs, apprehensive, skittish. That was a good sign. Tony fluttered off of Mrs. Toennis' shoulder and landed on mine. I stayed cool, hoping to come away with at least one ear. He continued to remain silent.

When we got to the living room, he took off for the mantle, landing between a set of family pictures and an arrangement of china knickknacks. He sat there looking at us. I waited for him to pronounce some judgment, but he remained silent. I turned toward Mrs. Toennis and saw that she was sitting calmly, paying no attention to him. Finally, he spoke.

"Hello mother. Hello mother. Who's the kid? Hello Mickey. Hello Mickey. Awk-k-k. Dumb dog! [then a pause] Poor Mickey. Poor Mickey. Hel-l-l-o. Hel-l-l-o. Dumb dog!"

It wasn't much, considering the epic saga of his previous exploits, but it was enough for me. I never doubted her again. "He's a little tired," she explained. "He's been flying around all day."

Mrs. Toennis was eccentric, but she wasn't rich. The Bensons were rich, but they weren't eccentric. Eventually I learned that you could find both without searching in distant realms.

Their name was Brooks. I went to high school with their son and dated their daughter. Actually, I only dated her once; that was, as it turned out, more than enough. I had seen her at parties, but not often, since we moved in different circles. She attended a private school with the word "Academy" in its name, while most of my female friends attended the more down-to-earth Regina.

Jeannie Brooks seemed nice enough. She was more reserved than her brother David, a high school swimmer with an athlete's body, rich boy's wardrobe, surfer's blond hair, and sailor's morals. The more I saw of his crowd, the more I came to realize that there really was such a thing as middle-class morality.

The rich girls were as loose as the boys, particularly when they escaped the watchful eyes of their parents. They never sat on chairs when there was an available lap, and they never let good liquor go to waste. They were as close to the Hollywood of dream and legend as one could get in Cincinnati.

Except for Jeannie. She seemed somewhat jaded at times, but she had manners to match her good taste. I remember her cheeks.

They were rosy and English. Her hair was chestnut brown. Her school uniform consisted of a silk blouse and a pleated skirt, and the skirt was always meticulously pressed.

Her brother suggested I ask her out. Eventually I did. She lived beyond the city limits, in the village of (as God is my judge) Loveland. When the date finally arrived and I showed up at her door, her brother suggested we double-date with him and his friend Patricia Cantwell. Patricia's father, Randolph Cantwell, was a corporate attorney. Her mother had inherited (and promptly sold) a company that manufactured cardboard packaging materials. They liked to spend their summer afternoons at the Cincinnati Country Club; their daughter liked to spend hers with David Brooks. The evenings, too, I learned, and if the chance presented itself, the mornings as well.

This was an inauspicious beginning to the evening, since I feared that Patricia and David might go into an unending clinch and Jeannie and I would be uncomfortable and, eventually, embarrassed. David was combing his hair in the bathroom, and I went in to talk to him about it. Since the bathroom was nearly the size of my bedroom at home, I knew that he wouldn't feel crowded.

I closed the door to speak with him in private, and he promptly turned on the water while continuing to comb his hair. I asked him why he had done that. "I thought you might want some privacy," he said. He figured that I was going to use the toilet, and he was muffling any potential sounds so that his mother (who was in the next room) would remain ignorant of my activities. I found this thoughtful but a little strange.

I told him I just wanted to talk and asked him whether or not he was sure that he wanted to double-date. He looked at me, paused for a minute, and then smiled. "So you've got big plans, is that it?"

"No, not at all," I answered, "but I thought you might."

"OK, yeah, OK," he said. "Why don't you go out with Jeannie by yourself, and we'll all get together later on."

"That sounds good," I said, wondering where he and Patricia might be going in the meantime.

I checked my hair in the bathroom mirror, opened the door, stepped into the living room, and found myself in the middle of a Faulkner novel. David's elder brother was named John. John was the silent, haunted type. He was playing chess with himself in the corner, using a pivoting board. I walked toward him, thought about offering some pleasantry, saw the serpent stare when he looked up at me, and decided to move on.

The younger brother was sitting in a chair, handling a football. He was too little to get a good grip on it, but he slid it back over his right hand and then slammed it into his left. He did this several times without looking up. I walked past his chair, commented on the ball (it was a Rawlings), and waited for some response. He didn't look up. Both he and the elder brother seemed to be seething with anger for no particular reason.

The father was not in evidence. I never met the father. I never even saw pictures of the father. Jeannie was still upstairs getting dressed, and I continued to pace. David came out of the bathroom, slipped on a jacket and scarf, said goodbye, and promptly left. Just then the mother got out of her chair and approached me.

To say that she looked strange was to understate the case considerably. She was dressed all in dark, clashing colors—blues, browns, and black, with forest green stockings and a brown fortune-teller's fringed shawl. Two statements issued from her lips. The first was, "You're Schwartz."

I was always taught that it was impolite to refer to someone by his or her last name. Even the nuns used our first names when correcting us, usually eliding the first and last name with the command of the moment: "RichardSchwartzgetbackinyourseat!" I gave her the benefit of the doubt by figuring that this was some kind of rich thing. Perhaps this was the way they referred to each other at their private clubs. "Ah, Brooks, old fellow, how *is* that Madeira?"

The second thing she said was far more problematic. She ushered me to the table, a gnarled slab of mahogany designed for the dining room but placed for some occult reason in the center of the living room. Above it was an antique candelabra. The metal needed a good polishing, and it was lightly, but noticeably, cobwebbed. Looking down at a dish in the center of the table, she asked, "Would you like a lichee nut?"

I paused to think about that a second when she suddenly interrupted my chain of thought, saying, "They're not really lichee nuts, of course, but we can pretend. . . ."

The Twilight Zone. With images of Fu Manchu's daughter hallucinating under the press of hunger or the effects of some bad opium. "Thanks," I said, "but I've just eaten."

I hadn't, and it was a stupid thing to say, but how do you summon up a good response to something as unexpected as the invitation to play the imitation lichee nut game with your date's mother, who looks like Esmeralda in the penny arcade fortune booth at Coney Island?

"Well then, how about some tea?"

"Thanks," I said, "but I really don't care for any."

I did like tea, but feared its diuretic effects, particularly if Jeannie took longer than I thought she might. I had already logged some time in the Brooks's toilet, with David running the water for background, and I didn't want the lichee nut lady thinking I had some kind of problem.

"All right then," she said. "What time do you intend to return with my daughter?"

"I'm not sure," I answered. "We're going to meet David and Patricia later." No sooner did I say it than I realized that David had failed to tell me when or where.

"I see," she said. The notion that we would be with her son provided scant comfort. Perhaps because she knew Patricia. Perhaps because she knew David.

I looked toward the stairs, wondering when Jeannie would appear and release me from the inquisition, but I had at least another ten minutes to wait. During that time, I was asked about my plans for college and my plans for life. I was asked about my parents and my parents' parents. I was even offered tea a second time, though the lichee nut offer was not renewed.

Eventually Jeannie appeared. Far from being my saviour, she was nervous and harried. Something had gone wrong with her wardrobe or her makeup. Perhaps David had said something to her about Patricia and our proposed meeting. Whatever had happened, it had not been good.

"Hi," I said, "good to see you. You look very nice."

"Let's go," she said abruptly.

The little brother was still clutching his football, and the elder brother was still playing chess. When I looked over, he was pondering a move, holding on to the top of a rook, being careful to abide by the rules even though he was playing against himself. I turned to say goodbye to the mother, but she was already gone. I turned to open the door for Jeannie, and she was already opening it for herself.

She's upset, I thought, but at least she's not crazy. At least she doesn't have a secret life that is the stuff of gothic fiction. At least she's borderline normal. Not that I was expecting the perfect evening or even a very pleasant one, but at least I was leaving behind me the lichee nut house and its assorted occupants.

It was cold that night, and there was a thin coating of ice on the cement pathway between the house and the driveway. "Here, let me help you," I said, reaching out to offer an arm against which she might balance herself.

"I'm all right," she said, curtly. She then took two uncertain steps which seemed to reinforce her resolve. She took two more, and suddenly her legs went out from under her. It was a clean fall, straight up and straight down—flat on her bottom. I tried to help her up. She looked at me, her eyes widening, and then she suddenly began to scream.

"Shit! God*damn* it! Son . . . of . . . a . . . *bitch!*" she said, the decibel level rising with each word. Before she even finished with the "Goddamn it," I knew that I had somehow misjudged her personality. Then she spoke again.

"Listen, Schwartz, if you ever mention this . . . to anyone, I'll . . . I'll . . ."

"Don't worry," I said. "I won't."

Again with the single name business. I concluded that it must have been a family convention. I suppose my recounting of this episode constitutes a breaking of my promise to her, but that part of my story happened nearly forty years ago and I feel some obligation to tell the truth about what happened that evening, and besides, I *have* changed her name. Needless to say, the date was an uphill struggle from that point on, and there was never a second one. I don't remember the specific details of the evening, but I remember that we did eventually run into David and Patricia. He took one look at us and decided not to ask us how our date went. I took one look at Patricia and the state of her remaining lipstick and didn't ask them either.

It wasn't so much that I ran back to my own neighborhood in horror, so much as that I was confused. At the time, I figured their money made them harder to satisfy than the rest of us. This accounted for their world-weariness and self-indulgence, their impatience and their false pride. Then I figured maybe they were too inbred, like the Hapsburgs or some of the people from mountain hollows and tobacco road towns in Kentucky. Finally, it all began to come into focus. After sorting through a succession of possibilities, there was one, solid conclusion that I could draw from the experience, a conclusion that linked these key members of the family of man. When a member of either inbred group's ass hit the ice, the resulting expletives could always be counted on to be more or less the same. While the rich might be different from us, there were always circumstances under which they could somehow manage to act in precisely the same ways as the poor.

The Cincinnati *Times Star* regularly included a section on debutantes and their families, a section whose contents seemed more remote than the activities of the inhabitants of distant planets. There was never a story, but instead a simple listing of august presences. It has been said that the middle class works while the aristocracy's function is simply to *be*. That was certainly confirmed by the editorial policy of the *Times-Star*. I remember a particular photo spread, one involving a costume party at a country club. A rich boy is standing in Civil War officer's dress and droopy artificial mustache next to a woman with a period hairdo in a southern belle's gown clutching a purse. They each look like characters out of a bad play. The caption read: "Jeffrey Curtin III looks on as Bethany Harmon holds a beaded reticule." A beaded reticule? Give me Jeannie Brooks sitting on the ice and raising her curses to the night sky.

4

1952

Tuesday in the Park with John

Years later, this assistant professor in a Dunn and Company tweed jacket with a full-bent billiard pipe told us that the woods are actually a threshold symbol. "They represent," he said, "that area of life that is beyond normal experience. 'One' enters the woods to have magic experiences, dangerous experiences, unique experiences. The woods are the locus of romanticism, just as they are the setting of Romance, romantics skipping the eighteenth century and returning to the renaissance in an exercise of literary 'grandfatherism.' The woods are the world beyond the protective walls of the medieval city; they are the darkness at the edge of the village; they are the world of faëry, the world from which 'ladies' must be rescued; they are the world of imminent threat and looming evil."

Somehow we had known it all along. We had learned it firsthand, and it wasn't always very romantic. Our woods were at the bottom of Fenwick Avenue: a few hundred acres of marsh, scrub pine, and hardwood, running along parallel, abrupt slopes bisected by a city park. They were five minutes away by foot, less than a minute by bike. Before the tract houses came, I could see them from both my front and back yards.

The north slope provided insulation for a railroad spur that serviced a chemical plant. Too steep for play and too thin for exploration, it also had a way of attracting bums drawn by the railroad tracks and the leftover grandstand food from a Babe Ruth League baseball field adjoining the chemical plant. The south slope, on the other hand, was ours, and we spent every dry summer day in its midst. To the east was a swamp, covered with emerald green slime and brimming with life. It supplied the tadpoles which were placed occasionally in the girls' shelter house sink or toilet bowl by boys hoping to evoke a response of terror or disgust. (The uniform reaction of the girls: mature indifference.) The woods above the marshy area were too steep for effective play and were used only as a shortcut to some of my friends' homes. Because those woods were little used, they served as a convenient hiding place when the park counsellors or police were looking for us.

Not that the police came calling with any degree of frequency, but if they were in the area and if there were some plausible basis for assuming they were there because of us, the woods above the marsh offered a good place to hide. The police (and one or two firemen) *were* there on at least one occasion—a dust-dry fifth or sixth of July when some leftover cherry bombs and M-8os were set off near the softball field and fears arose concerning a possible fire.

The south slope to the west was home—stretching from Fenwick Avenue and the entrance to Fenwick Park on the east all the way to Cincinnati Gardens and its parking lots on the west. Beneath it was the park with its pool, shelter house, swings, slides, monkey bars, parking lot, and softball field. Behind it was a line of residential housing, separated from the woods by green backyards and six-foot hurricane fencing.

The south slope woods were divided into three major sections. The first consisted of heavy vines, capable of sustaining the weight of several preadolescent boys. With the sloping ground beneath us and the flatter land above, we would get a running start, clutch the main vine, and then swing out into space, our feet high above the thorns and nettles in the undergrowth below.

At one point on the top of the hill, the thorn bushes were so dense that a fort was constructed at their center, a fort accessible through a maze of vines, roots, and thorny branches. The fort itself consisted of little more than some circular, levelled ground capable of containing three or four boys. The thorn fort functioned more as a curiosity than a haven, since entering it (and, hence, ex-

Fenwick Park (two views). The pool is now filled in, covered by a basketball court.

iting it) was a slow and complicated process. It was actually a transparent maze. While an enemy might see you at its center and be unable to find the way in, it was impossible for you to find your way out without revealing both the exit route and your approaching physical presence to the enemy. In the meantime, you could be pelted with rocks, mud, or water balloons virtually at will. Some said that it would be useful at night—you could sleep inside of it without fear of being surprised by bums—but no one, to my knowledge, ever expressed an actual wish to sleep on the ground, uncovered, surrounded by thorn bushes. When evening fell, we wanted our roofs, beds, refrigerators, and tiny, black-and-white TV screens.

The center section of the woods contained a four-foot-square wooden shed that some unknown but skilled person had once taken the time and trouble to construct. We called it the BB gun shack, because older boys occasionally occupied it and used the light slits provided by its builder to support the barrels of their BB guns. Again, it was not a particularly secure fort, because it was small, dark, cramped, and essentially uninhabitable. Once inside, you were secure for as long as you could stand to be there, while your enemy could simply wait outside for you and pummel you the moment you opened the door. Its chief purpose seemed to be to provide shelter during the rain for somebody looking for a quiet, dry place to get drunk. In this regard, the older boys sketched out more exotic explanations for its existence, most of them involving acts of a sexual nature. They spun out assorted scenarios for our instruction and amazement, but since the BB gun shack had a dirt floor and was smaller than the back seat of an average sedan, we received their suggestions with some skepticism.

Our real fort was at the western end of the woods and enjoyed a series of distinct advantages which we recounted with pride. The fort proper was a large hole dug out of the clay, approximately nine feet square and four feet deep. Across the top was positioned a large sheet of galvanized steel which had been abandoned at a construction site behind the local dairy. On the south side of the fort was a pit in which we would build fires, the heat from which was conducted through the steel roof, resulting in a primitive form of centralized heating. The Romans heated the floor; we heated the ceiling. The woods were dense at the immediate rear of the fort, but just beyond them was open park area, so that escapes of various kinds could be effected.

Inside the woods, approximately 150 feet in front of the fort, was a hill of strategic importance. To the east of the hilltop was the trail running back through the length of the south slope woods. To the west was a trail that ran down the hillside and around to our fort. Thus, the hilltop served as a perfect lookout post, from which one could observe any suspicious activity to the east. To the northwest, one could observe the fort itself and any possible threats to its occupants. Thus, a guard was always posted on the hill to provide protection for those of us spending time in the fort proper. One of our number paced carefully, stopping at one of three stations, looking out in key directions, and reporting a regular "all clear," while the rest of us read comic books or drank grape Kool-Aid from glass milk bottles.

One of the major decisions we always faced was whether or not to cover the corrugated steel roof with dirt, thus camouflaging the fort. This option was balanced against the alternative of leaving the roof exposed, but being able to slide it backward or forward with ease in the case of an enemy attack. These two options were debated endlessly, with individual decisions usually made on whim.

The fort had one major advantage and one major drawback. It was located no more than two hundred yards from the field adjoining Gerry Gelb's house, so that we could always go there for drinks, cookies, or better shelter when the need arose. The disadvantage was that Gerry's neighbor on the other side of the street (Rhonda Lane) was a fisherman who routinely cleaned his catch in the woods, a few minutes' walk from our fort. Moving the fort was not an option, since the location was ideal. Our only choice was to endure the smells of fish heads and fish guts on those hot summer days when he had been particularly successful.

Gerry's house was also my consummate ideal, at least until I was thirteen or fourteen. When I was four or five, my favorite

book in the world had been *The New House in the Forest.* It told of
a perfect family that builds a perfect house in the perfect setting—
near the city, but still deep in the woods. Its materials are perfect
bricks, perfect tiles, perfect plaster, and perfect boards of perfect
pine and oak. Its water supply is an adjoining lake, always fresh,
never murky, filled with beautiful, shiny fish, as happy and hand-
some as fish can be. Surrounded by wildlife and towering trees, it
is nonetheless close enough to town to provide dad a job to help
him pay the mortgage, purchase the flowers and candy he brings
to mom and the humidors of tobacco he smokes in his pipe.
(There is no talk of any mortgage in the story, but I was shrewd
enough to figure out that dad needed a paycheck, because no one
in *The New House in the Forest* would have hunted and eaten any of
the creatures who were their neighbors, and certain things aren't
free: the gasoline for dad's peppy but comfortable sedan, the cardi-
gans that he wears when he sits beside the fire, or the vet services
for his unnamed red setter, who greets him at the door each time
he returns and shares the warmth of his fire, sprawled on a brown,
oval rug at his feet.)

Gerry's house *was* the house in the forest. Although there were
other houses beyond it to the west, it adjoined the woods on the
east and was separated from them by nothing more than a small
meadow in which we sometimes played football. I often thought
about what it would be like to actually live on the edge of the
woods like him. Our house was farther from the woods than Gerry's by a single city block, an unacceptable distance by any reasonable measure. I always felt special things at his house, and my
sense of wonder somehow managed to block out the nearby
traffic, the chemical plant across the way (with its periodic explo-
sions), the Culligan water softener business at the end of Gerry's
street, the bums, the railroad tracks, and the other reminders of
the presence of civilization on the woods' periphery.

Simpler, safer times, they say. Simple enough that we had no
hesitation in arming ourselves to the teeth. Multiple-shot BB
guns were common but not omnipresent, since they had to be pro-
tected from moisture, dust, and mud and set down carefully

against some stable, dry, relatively clean object whenever we wanted to pursue other activities. They also had to be carried. A sling over the shoulder seemed pretentious, and sweaty hands on the barrel could lead to rust. There were only so many ways a BB gun could be held and carried, most of them inconvenient. A Red Ryder was hardly as heavy as a Browning automatic rifle, but sometimes it was just more fun to carry a stick. You could whip a stick through the air and listen to the hissing sound. You could snap it against the side of trees. You could snap it against somebody's butt. You could throw it away when you got tired of it, knowing that you could always find a new one.

Hatchets, which we regularly carried, could be slipped between our belts and jeans, and there were no moving parts to protect. Knives were carried in cases attached to our belts. My special knife had a raised portrait of Daniel Boone on its leather sheath. It featured a six-inch blade, sharpened lovingly on my father's Carborundum block, its box (and later, my knife's sheath) redolent with the warm and comforting smell of fresh Three-in-One oil.

The thought now of a group of twelve-year-olds so armed, playing alone in a woods accessible from several directions by potential deviants and miscreants, indicates how different our lives were then. Now my mind races to the thought of possible accidental woundings, maimings, and worse and the attendant lawsuits and broken lives, not to the fact that such things never did happen (at least to us), as we played and learned and grew. *What* we learned with all that weaponry might give the concerned pious some pause. Perhaps one of the lessons was that we *should* have been able to play in our neighborhood and the woods that were a part of it without fear, our sense of fear being moderated by a reasonable degree of prudence and a proper amount of weaponry. I say "perhaps," because we never thought of it. Playing in the woods was what we did, and its proximity to us was a gift. Beyond that, our thoughts never strayed.

Our work and play in the woods coexisted with the activities in the park below. The counsellors were college students on their summer break, paid by the hour to maintain order and direct the park's programs. To us, they seemed tall and old—nineteen at least, possibly as ancient as twenty-two. They issued the paddles, balls, and nets from a large oak chest with an imposing Yale lock. They sold the craft materials: copper sheets pounded into the shape of ashtrays with ball-peen hammers, gimp from which to fashion plastic lanyards, colored elastic loops with which to make potholders.

Lanyards were a favorite creation. The counsellors' help was usually needed to set the metal clasp and start the first half-inch or so of line. When we reached an appropriate length, we sought their help a second time to start the "box" through which the necklace line passed, then a third time to complete the project. The weaving required a stationary object, to which the clasp could be attached while the line was held reasonably taut and the weaving done. By general agreement, the ideal object was a hurricane fence. The clasp could be attached to it, and one could look through it while working, thus alleviating boredom.

Thus, at any one time, the park swimming pool was surrounded by lanyard makers, all standing next to the fence, weaving their multicolored gimp and occasionally pausing to look at the swimmers or the hill and woods above the pool. An observer who neither understood the method nor the purpose of the activity would assume that a set of young people were being punished for some infraction and forced to stand against a fence, performing an activity analogous to the breaking of rocks or digging of dirt.

The making of crafts presented the usual challenge to parents—the need to stare approvingly and express loving gratitude for a superfluous object. How many potholders can the average middle-class household absorb? How many furniture groupings will accommodate a copper ashtray with innumerable decorative bumps? How many adults have the occasion to wear a whistle on a plastic necklace and, assuming the need, how many wish to possess them in multiple colors and box styles?

Each craft had its attractions. The lanyard—being the most complicated—enabled you to intimidate the young with your skill and acuity. The ashtray afforded the opportunity to pound loudly for an extended period of time in a useful endeavor. The potholder gave you the chance to work with the wooden frame surrounded by finishing nails tapped into its periphery. The feel of the nail-heads was somehow gratifying. (MLA sex-and-psych analysts, where are you?) The interlaced pattern was simple so that the activity was useful without being completely mindless. Repairs could easily be made, colors substituted, patterns altered. When you tired of work, you could play with the materials themselves. The loops were generally placed beside the frame in a large pile which could be gathered in a single grasp, lifted, and squeezed, the texture and elasticity of the material then being felt and experienced. Tightening your grip and then loosening it, the loops sprang back to life, falling over and through your fingers like cloth slinkies or escaping, circular worms.

Crafts could be done when there were too few people for team sports. They could also be done in the rain, in which case the lanyard clasps were attached to the grillwork on the shelter house windows. That was a poor substitute for a section of hurricane fence, but the bad weather afforded other opportunities. The indoor pounding of ashtrays, for example, offered the attraction of annoying the Ping-Pong players next to the picnic tablework spaces within the shelter house.

The favored team sports were basketball and baseball. Volleyball was a poor third, and soccer had not yet been discovered. Badminton was an unattractive alternative, because the park budget did not permit the purchase of racquets. Instead, the plastic (non-feathered) shuttlecock was struck with large wooden paddles. These paddles not only materially changed the nature of the game, but they also offered an irresistible temptation to sore losers to use them on the butts of their opponents, games inevitably deteriorating into opportunities for abuse and humiliation.

As I think back over the long summer days spent in the park, three occurrences in particular stand out. The first was the unexpected appearance at a softball game of a blood relative of a member of the Brooklyn Dodgers. Visiting friends in Cincinnati, he

The Fenwick Park ballfield. The woods where we played are along the third base line.

came to the park that day and was persuaded to join in our game. He played left field and—carrying his famous relative's name—seemed obliged to do all that he could to play above his ability.

Watching him tear up his arms, diving for foul fly balls among the undergrowth, and seeing him covered in dust after sliding into second base when the third out had already been made at first, I realized the burden of a famous name. I also gained some appreciation of the importance of character—more, by the way, than I had learned in religion class. By the eighth inning, he was both battered and exhausted. When he dropped an easily caught fly ball, we were all somehow reassured. He had already given more than anyone could reasonably expect. Worst of all, he carried the name of Roy Rogers' wife, Dale. It wasn't exclusively a woman's name then, but it was close enough to being so to evoke additional sympathy from a group of boyish twelve-year-olds.

The second event came later that summer, when one of the retarded kids relieved himself in the swimming pool, removing his trunks and passing a floater that lingered on the surface, horrified the counsellors, and resulted in the closing, draining, cleansing, and refilling of the pool, a process that extended over several days and added to the poignancy of the event.

The retarded kids were brought to the park two or three days a week and seated at a set of picnic tables on the hill, just above the slides, where they were taught by special teachers and counsellors. They were never taunted or teased, in part because their separation from the rest of us was systematically maintained. When accidents or problems occurred, the response was generally sympathetic, the pool incident being a prime instance. The sense of empathy ran so deep that the occurrence was seldom mentioned, despite the fact that it was uppermost in everyone's mind for days. The only experience I could compare it with was the response of the students in my high school to the plight of a freshman who was accompanied by his mother for the first day of school. This was so horrid, so embarrassing, that even the toughs and borderline felons refused to comment on it.

The third event was more personal. This time I wasn't watching from center field or the other side of the pool fence. I was involved directly, and there was no way to escape the confrontation. We were playing football. What was unusual for us was that we actually had eleven players on each team, and, though our jerseys were mismatched, we all wore helmets and shoulder pads. It was a real game, as real as they got. I was playing left guard. I tackled the other team's halfback twice in the opening minutes of the game. Nothing dirty and nothing really memorable. What happened was that he ran into me, and I put my arms around his legs and held on until he fell.

Outraged by the fact that he had been brought down by someone noticeably smaller than him (the positions played bearing little or no relation to size or skill), he threatened me, telling me that if I tackled him again I would have to answer to him later. I knew that I couldn't simply let him run by, so I told him that if he didn't want to be tackled by me he should run around the other end. My teammates took this as a flip threat rather than a simple statement of fact (as I intended it to be), and they were surprised to hear it from me, since the smaller boys were seen as normal prey for bullies and they were expected to retreat whenever possible. (I was the second smallest boy on the field, after Donnie Reischauer, who was playing right end.)

I didn't know what else to say. I could hardly promise not to tackle him. I knew that he was more angry at himself than at me, but that was his problem, even though he wanted to make it mine. On the next play, he ran right for me. Instead of hedging my bets, waiting for him to come forward, waiting for the tackle and center to crowd against me and share in the tackle as well as the guilt, I stepped forward and tackled him in the backfield. I don't really know why I did it. It was part instinct, part anger, part pride, and, I thought at the time, part stupidity. Regardless of the reason, it was enough for him. He told me he would wait for me after the game, and he promised to beat me mercilessly. He also took a certain pleasure in announcing it early so that I could think about it for the next three and a half quarters.

Several of my teammates told me to leave, one mentioning the fact that the halfback had beaten up another boy the week before. He had bruised his nose, cut his cheek just below his eye, and then bent his arm behind his back until it nearly broke. They told me that everyone would understand, that the bully (his name was John Goble) was also rich, so that even if I managed to hurt him in some way (a possibility carrying very long odds) his family would make trouble for mine.

I thought about it for the rest of the first quarter (tackling him again, this time with the help of our left end) and came to the conclusion that I had to hold my ground. What finally convinced me was the fact that, though he was much bigger than I was, he was nearly a year younger. When you are twelve, age is everything.

The shame of being beaten by an eleven-year-old was harder to contemplate than the difficulty of preventing it.

There were two other things that angered me. One was his wealth and the manner in which he displayed it. The second was the fact that he had a retarded brother whom he never mentioned. The family kept the brother in the house throughout the year, no matter what the season. He lived on the second floor of their large house on Quatman Avenue, and he could sometimes be seen waving from the middle front window. He didn't have Down's syndrome. His facial features were normal; he looked like a younger version of his older brother, John. At least that was the consensus from those who had seen him.

I didn't understand why they kept the younger brother locked up. Other retarded kids came to the park all the time. What really bothered me, though, was the fact that Johnny Goble had somehow decided to disown him. I never had a brother myself, and the way that Johnny treated his was, I thought, mean.

After the football game was over, I approached him and asked him if he still wanted to fight me. He was standing on the side of the hill, between the road and steps that led out of the park, blocking my way. He told me that he didn't want to fight me, what he wanted to do was beat me, beat me in a way I would never forget, beat me so that the rest of my teammates could see what happened to little smartasses who thought they could tackle John Goble. Then he paused for a second, smiled, and offered me one last chance to run away. "Go ahead, you little chickenshit," he said, "run home to your mother while you still can. I know that's what you want to do." By then, the rest of the players had come over from the ballfield. I could feel their eyes on the back of my head.

I remember saying only one thing. I told him that if I fought him I didn't want to hear him complain later that I had beaten up somebody younger than me, a comment that brought peals of instant laughter. Some of his friends laughed, called me names, and urged him to make me pay for saying that.

No one came forward to help me. I hadn't expected them to. I stared at him for an eternity that was probably somewhere between three and five seconds. Then I stepped forward and leaped on him, knocking him to the ground. Sitting on his stomach, looking down at his mouth, now open in shock, I proceeded to do something that I never really thought I could—I beat the living shit out of him.

I probably hit him thirty or forty times before I stopped, adopting the right swing/left swing model so common in the five-o'clock westerns on *Six-Gun Theater*. I didn't hit very hard, because I couldn't hit very hard, but I managed to keep hitting him in the same places, mostly in his cheeks, below his eyes, but sometimes in his ears and on the side of his neck. The longer I hit, the redder he got, a combination of emotion and the effects of my blows.

His astonishment turned into pain, which then turned into fear. I was weeping uncontrollably, probably as part of an attempt to release my own fear, and I remember crying out, asking him to stop, to end it, though all he was doing was receiving my blows. He never cried, but he also never struck back. In a state somewhere between frenzy and ecstasy, I continued to hit him. By now his left ear was beet red and puffy. I thought that was good, very good.

When his friends called me a bully, I got up and stood aside, allowing him to rise, though I feared that he might now hit me. The realization that I had actually beaten him was still hours away. He didn't say a word, to anyone. Instead, he turned, walked up the steps and out of the park. He went home, as it turned out, and then promptly returned, carrying an expensive piece of steak in the palm of his hand, which he periodically applied to his left eye and left cheek. I had seen meat used in that way a hundred times in cartoons. That was the only time in my life I ever saw it happen with real people. The family had sent their sirloin rather than their lawyers.

When John Goble returned, he stood on the edge of the park, watching. We didn't know why. An after-the-fact assertion of something? An order from his mother that that was the way Gobles behaved? He just stood there, watching us, holding onto the meat, pressing it against his cheek and eye. We saw him there, stared at him a moment, and then decided to ignore him, spending a few minutes on the monkey bars, before we went up the hill and into the woods to spend the rest of the afternoon at our fort.

He never tried to bother me again, and I never said anything to him about the beating or about his carrying around a piece of meat. The incident seemed to change him, not completely, but a little. It made him nicer, easier to play with, though he never became a friend.

I saw his retarded brother once. It was about a year later. I was walking back from the drug store up at Quatman and Montgomery, and I happened to look up at the second floor windows of the Goble house. I waved at the little boy, and he put his hand up against the window and looked down at me. His name was Bill.

5

1953

The Dance

There were two kinds, of course, the dance in the school gym and the real dance, the dance between boys and girls, the dance that never ends. Before the dance came the investiture, and that was a project unto itself.

The uniform always changes, and it is always dictated by current fashion, which is to say it is dictated by peer pressure more powerful than a jackhammer operating at full throttle. In the 1950s, that pressure was multiplied exponentially, because the fifties combined their particular flair for fashion with an overpowering need to be in the swim without causing ripples. The entire country was a Clearasil-smeared adolescent nervously staring into a full-length mirror of self-doubt. We all wanted to exude uniqueness so long as we also looked exactly like everyone else.

For boys in Norwood, there were two mandatory stops. The first was Max's, a clothing store at the north end of the pike which later moved to the Swifton Shopping Center. Before the shopping malls and the strip malls came, the pike (Montgomery Road from the Point to Dana Avenue) brought buyers to Norwood. The stores along the pike (and the industrial plants to its east and northwest) created Norwood. There are still stores there, but they are all plastic boxes with the bright but tiresome logos of the same familiar chains. In the fifties, the stores were unique. If you were in need and committed to serious shopping, your only choice was to go to the pike. Years later, when other alternatives presented themselves, the population of Norwood fell by a full one-third.

Max's carried a full range of men's clothing from socks to suits, but we only went there for shirts, the shirts with high, spreading collars and necks that formed a *V*. We wanted the same shirts that Bob Cummings wore on his TV show: Bob Cummings, bachelor photographer, surrounded by leggy models with deep V-neck blouses and snug sweaters. Bob Cummings, brought to you by Winston (which "tastes good, like a cigarette should"). Bob Cummings, enduring Hollywood star and permanent fixture, with champagne glass in hand, at Mocambo, the Brown Derby, and the Trocadero. Bob Cummings, our role model.

Each season, the color of choice changed, but that color was always identified by an exotic adjective. Not just green, but mint green; not just blue, but Tahoe blue; not off-white, but eggshell white. Gunmetal gray, lemon yellow, and the purple to end all purples: heliotrope. And you would actually walk into the store, step up to the counter, look the nice Jewish salesman in the eye as he clutched the ends of the tape measure around his neck, and say, "Heliotrope." And your expression wouldn't change, and the expression of the salesman wouldn't change. He always knew just what you wanted because he knew what everybody wanted: heliotrope. That's why he ordered his shirts by the gross.

Max's was the answer for shirts, but you would never buy pants there. Pants were always hand-tailored. For them, you went to Sherman Avenue Tailors and its owner, Freddy Zorndorf. Freddy's store sat in a location so perfect that other retailers could only suppress their envy, rearrange the merchandise in their windows, order new fabric lines, and hope for better days: Sherman Avenue Tailors was midway between the pike and Norwood High School.

Freddy's shop was nondescript. His samples sat on a table near the front window, and his walls were decorated with old posters that touted the importance of hand-tailored garments and reduced the human form and its draping to a discrete set of lines, arrows, and measurements. Most of Freddy's business was in pants, and the design parameters were clear. The first requirement was that the pants be pegged (narrowed at the cuffs). Fourteen inches was standard, anything smaller too extreme. Older high school boys preparing for the onset of middle age might go to fifteen inches (some seeing it as an announcement of advanced maturity), but anything beyond that was out of the question. Pants with sixteen-inch cuffs were only worn by people who had bought readymades or who spent their lives in places like Xenia or Zanesville operating farm machinery.

The sides of the trousers were cut in one of three fashions: with a single welt, a double welt, or a double welt with a separate color down the center. The latter was generally pink with black welts and was favored by those who purchased beer by the quart and Vitalis by the gallon. Double-welted black pants with pink stripes were worn with tee shirts with twisted packs of Luckies at the shoulder. They were worn by the people our girlfriends' parents ordered their daughters to avoid.

Double welts were doable, but a bit over the top, particularly when you were already specifying reverse flaps with pearl snaps for the back pockets. The latter, a touch of early Roy Rogers, had to be balanced by a conservative, single welt. The pocket flaps were triangular in shape, not oblong, and, while the pearl snaps were de rigueur for the ultrahip, it was possible to get by with buttons instead: a nice understatement.

The material of choice was sharkskin, a hard-wearing wool capable of standing up to all of the challenges its young wearers were capable of posing. Freddy understood all of this. First, he took the measurements, then he walked you through the design details. The choice of fabric was nearly an afterthought.

"Cuff . . . fourteen?"

"Right."

"Single welt, right?"

"Right."

"Pockets . . . reverse flaps?"

"Right."

"Buttons or snaps?"

"Snaps."

The pike, facing south. The smoke shop and Max's were at the approximate site of the paint ad; the street is wider now.

Sherman Avenue Tailors. Where the tailor shop once displayed its trade in the windows, new businesses now operate.

"Pearl?"

"Right."

Five words and you had specified a garment the significance of which would require two or three volumes to describe and explain to a Martian visitor. Freddy was a gem. He understood the tailoring business, and he understood thirteen-year-old boys. And he was a pure pro—the sort who could outfit James Bond and look comfortable doing it. He could even look comfortable outfitting us. The best thing of all was that he never asked the dreaded question, "And what side do you wear your pants on?" in front of your parents. One day I was in Freddy's shop with a friend of mine named John Parnell. John was getting measured, and Freddy asked him "the question" very quietly. John hesitated, not understanding it. I tried to get his attention so I could coach him, but Freddy (not missing a beat) said, "Most people wear them on the left" and kept on writing. "Sounds good," John said.

Across the street from Norwood High School was the Norwood YMCA. The YMCA was the site for Friday night dances, dances we were forbidden to attend. Actually, we weren't forbidden to attend the dances. We were forbidden to join the YMCA.

It is a fair question to ask why. Because of rampant drug use at the dances? No, there was no drug use at the dances. Because of rampant alcohol abuse at the dances? No, there was occasional alcohol abuse at the dances, but it was confined to rear stairways and dark corners. Because pagan rites were enacted which involved the sacrifice of virginal fourteen-year-olds? No, there were no pagan rites enacted, though there were many virginal fourteen-year-olds. Why then? Because the Y was technically considered a religion, and, as good Catholics, we were not permitted to join any other religion than the pastor's.

This was all spelled out in the Baltimore catechism, which even specified some of the religious groups we were not permitted to join (such as the Y). We were forbidden from doing a great number of things. For example, we were not allowed to be hypnotized, since (we were told) that could result in the slow but inevitable loss of willpower, something which Catholics were required to possess in abundance and keep in constant, operable condition. Moreover, we were forbidden to join "secret societies."

"Now this is getting interesting," one of my classmates said, "secret societies" conjuring up images of pagan rites involving the sacrifice of virginal fourteen-year-olds. However, we were chagrined to discover the identity of some of these societies, the most notable of which was the Masons. Since that group sounded to us like a construction union, we had difficulty determining the reason why we were not permitted to join. Some of the older boys were in unions already anyway, and that didn't seem to bother the pastor. Another group was easier: the Odd Fellows, an organization that each of my classmates immediately vowed never to join. The very name suggested something less than manly, and, since our grip on manliness was tentative in the extreme, the joining of any group which might call that manliness into further question was unthinkable.

Still, there was the issue of those Friday night dances, and, with our pastors denying us a route that was legal and honorable, we were forced to seek out other means. Fortunately, this did not prove to be particularly difficult. In fact, there was only one element required to secure our access to the dances: the presence of a card-carrying member of the Norwood Y willing to facilitate our entry.

The street-clothes men's room (as opposed to the locker-room showers and toilets) was at the end of a back hallway on the lower ground level of the building. At the rear of the men's room was a window that opened onto the parking lot behind the building. The plan was simple. The legal member of the Y entered the building, showed his identification card to the officials at the door, got his hand stamped, looked around to check for suspicious observers, and then proceeded to the men's room. An experienced professional would stop first at one of the Ping-Pong tables and make diversionary small talk.

Once inside the toilet, he opened the back window and let us in from the rear parking lot. So much for the entry phase. The next step was a matter of real art. The stamp on the back of the mem-

The Norwood YMCA (two views). Above, the 1950s window entrance is now blocked by the new brick construction on the left. Below is the basement window to the men's room.

ber's left hand had to be transferred to the back of our left hands. This was accomplished by the application of a sufficient amount of spit to dampen and hence revitalize the ink, followed by the joining of the back of the hands in a single neat motion and the subsequent application of thirty seconds of pressure.

The juncture phase was important, because the hands had to be positioned to keep the image pointed in the proper direction. The stamp couldn't be upside down or at odd angles. Fading was expected by the guards at the gymnasium doors, but bad positioning could prove to be a dead giveaway.

The pressure phase was far more difficult. Too little pressure and the transfer did not take. Too much pressure and the hands began to tremble, thus risking a hopelessly smeared image. It all had to do with some muscle reflex, which was illustrated by a test motion. First, you stood next to the wall and placed the back of your hand against the wall, leaning into it and supporting as much of your weight as possible. After thirty seconds, you stepped away from the wall and let your hand fall to your side. Suddenly, magically, your hand began to rise. It was Newton's third law of motion for the hand (or something). Whatever it was, you had to watch out for some similar unanticipated, unwanted movement occurring when you had the back of your hand pressed against the ink-stained, spit-enlivened back of your friend's hand.

A master of the process could transfer his stamp three times, but there were few masters. Thus, when the image of red ink on a friend's hand began to fade to a hazardously faint degree, a volunteer (usually a stranger) was asked to take his place. Such individuals were usually cooperative, but they usually specified the requirement that they use their own spit and not yours.

The Y officials were notoriously lax in enforcing their own regulations, so that very little serious checking was done of the hand stamps. Moreover, since they were positioned at the top of the stairs on the second floor, outside the gym, they were not in a position to notice the fact that, for every two people who went into the first-floor men's room, four or five came out. We were able to multiply faster than the clowns emerging from the minibus at the Clyde Beatty circus.

Once into the gym, we could get on with the serious business of the dance: standing in the corner or on the side, talking, and looking at the girls. These girls were eminently watchable, since they were distinctly different from the girls we usually watched and sometimes dated. They were *Protestant* girls. And that, I hasten to point out, did not mean that they would meet our overtures with protests. On the contrary, it meant that they were not bound by the shackles of guilt, fear, ignorance, and misinformation that held us in thrall. They were living, breathing women-type creatures, with needs and desires and drives that had not been systematically removed from their psyches and bodies by surgeons in black robes with white wimples and white Roman collars. They were not like us. They were *real,* and it was our dream and privilege to find ourselves—every Friday night—in their company.

And we were ready to meet them on their own ground. After all, we were experienced fourteen-year-olds. We had been dating steadily for . . . weeks or even months. Of course, it was not always so. What little experience we had was the fruit of time and long labor. Come with me then to the time when this all began. Come with me to the sixth grade.

My days as an eleven-year-old were the best yet, and they started magically and unpredictably. It was a late summer afternoon, and the humidity lay on us like a warm down comforter. We were in Hunter Park, in northwest Norwood, talking to the older girls. Older meant fourteen in one case, thirteen in another, and fourteen meant sleeveless white blouses, open at the neck, with thin-strapped white bras visible from more angles than you could count.

As in most of these conversations, there were moments when the boys split off and talked among themselves, while the girls' heads came together in whispers and nervous laughter. Eventually, one of the girls came over and said something to my friend Jimmy Powers. Jimmy peeled off, walked to the side with her, talked for a few minutes, and then returned to our group. He put his hand on my shoulder, indicating that he wanted to say something to me privately.

I stepped back and said, "What?"

"Paula wants to kiss you," Jimmy said.

"What?" I answered.

"She wants to kiss you."

"She wants to kiss me?"

"Yes. Do it!"

"Why?"

"Because it'll be cool. Haven't you ever kissed a girl before, for god's sake?"

"Of course," I lied. Actually, it wasn't a lie, since aunts and older cousins qualified as girls, but the previous experiences had not been the kind that I wanted to relive. They all seemed to make you feel younger rather than older. "Go ahead, let Aunt Sally kiss you. It won't be so bad. Ah, look, he's bashful."

In this case, the offer to kiss Paula was an invitation to feel older—much older, as it turned out. Paula was nearly a foot taller than me (though she was sitting down now on a picnic bench), and she had been on real dates (at least I think she had). She had been kissed a thousand times, probably, and she would know just how to do it, while I would make a total fool of myself and look like some damned fifth grader, the kind of kid the nuns could still pull around by their ears.

Still, I looked at her and thought this might not be too bad of an idea. She had a trace of pink lipstick, and her brown hair was pinned up so you could see her long neck. Maybe I could just kiss her there, on the neck. That would be nice. But no, that would look silly. I'd have to go for all or nothing, and I couldn't mull it over, standing there with my toe in the dirt and my hands in my pockets.

"OK," I said and walked over toward the picnic bench.

"Hi," Paula said.

"Hi," I answered. "How are you?"

"I'm fine," she said. "How are *you*?"

"OK," I said, sitting down next to her, my chin close to her shoulder. "Mary Carol told Jimmy you wanted to see me."

"Yes," she said, leaning toward me. "Kiss me," she said. That's all, just "kiss me." I did, and the world changed forever.

It was soft and warm, and I remember that she smelled like fruit or candy. I think it was the lipstick combined with her shampoo. Apricots, maybe, or peaches, but not that distinct. I also remember, as she turned her head, feeling her bobby pins against the side of my head. Then she turned again, and I kissed her again. Eventually, she pulled her head back, looked at me like an older sister, and said, "I can see you've done this before."

Jimmy was impressed, the other boys were surprised, and I was gone, drifting somewhere into the ionosphere. Paula was smiling, her work complete. It was as if I had been inducted into some secret society and had just passed the entrance test. The other girls looked at me approvingly but proudly, as if I had just been taken captive by their side and they knew that I would never go back.

Once into the society, we took every opportunity available to reaffirm the society's foundational principles: a) kissing is good; b) more kissing is better. The kissing was both recreational and developmental, something to do and something to undergo. The person you were doing it with was less important than the fact that you were doing it. It was a preparation for life, not life itself, a year-long apprenticeship that would end and later be replaced with different behaviors with different rules, different assumptions, and different expectations.

There were three main kissing games that constituted the substance of a "kissing party." The first was Seven Minutes in Heaven, a game that had no particular rules other than the turning off of all lights for a period of seven minutes. The only challenge was to be positioned next to your prime object of desire at that moment when the lights came down. The second was Spin the Beanshooter, a vast improvement on the more traditional game of Spin the Bottle. In Spin the Beanshooter, the spinner kissed two people—the ones at whom the ends of the beanshooter pointed—rather than the single person to whom the neck of the bottle pointed. Spin the Beanshooter doubled your odds as well as your activities.

The third game was Slap, Kiss, and Hug. The person who was It sat with his back to the rest of the players as another person (often one of the senior, more maternal girls) asked, "Who do you want to do this to?" while making a symbolic gesture. Having selected the three people, the person who was It was then allowed to turn around and receive his instructions. "OK. Slap Mary Beth, kiss Susan, and hug Patty." The slaps were largely symbolic, the kisses and hugs more real, at least when administered by the boys.

All of these games required a series of characteristics possessed in abundance by sixth graders: a fundamental lack of understanding of the relationships between mature adults; a complete insensitivity to the awkwardness of the behavior; a sexual yearning satisfied by simple repetition rather than intensity or diversity—the belief that practice *is* perfect; and the ability to live absolutely in the moment, without jealousy, without a sense of past or future, and without a fear of personal, social, psychological, or physical consequences.

The sixth grade ended and with it all such crypto-romantic behaviors. Any prospect of serious attachments ended as well. Sports intervened. And high school. And cars. At least they intervened for the boys. For the girls, particularly the older girls, the behaviors sometimes continued in a new, more interesting form, for the girls were always more "mature," which is to say taller, less awkward, and more attuned to the nature and stakes of the dance.

We did not date until we could drive cars, our former girlfriends dating boys several years older in the interim. And we did eventually catch up, our cars providing the mobility and the symbols of maturity that made the catching up possible. In a given evening, we literally left hearth and home, exploring the world and our place in it. (In the course of a Cincinnati driving career, the norms changed. Initially, the goal was aimless wandering. This was later replaced with "time," as in "What kinda time didja make?") On any given evening, we could cover nearly half of the city, either accompanied by girls or meeting girls along the way as the occasion provided and always stopping at drive-up restaurants for further opportunities and sustenance.

Frisch's Big Boy—the source of the chain that has now been taken over by Marriott—was started by a Cincinnatian named Dave Frisch, and Dave Frisch's creation was an instant success. Frisch's featured four principal sandwiches, with the Big Boy, of course, as flagship offering, though it was then made with tartar sauce rather than the sweet goo that later replaced it. The original Big Boy was subtler, more adult, and much less like the penny-ante imitator that succeeded it, the Big Mac.

The second sandwich was the fish sandwich, the Filet of Sole, and in the beginning the sandwich actually consisted of sole. It was exquisite, again served with tartar sauce and shredded lettuce, but without a square of barely melted processed cheese or other glop. When the fisheries ran low on sole, Frisch's switched to "white fish." It was never the same, but it was far better than the competitors' products, which began to smell rancid and fishy the moment the sandwich cooled.

The third sandwich was the Brawny Lad: a steak sandwich on a rye bun with onion—very nice for those whose tastes ran in that direction and again far more subtle than its competitor, the Stromboli Steak Sandwich from LaRosa's, the pizzeria chain that still dominates the Queen City. The fourth was the Buddy Boy, Dave's only misfire, a ham sandwich on an oblong bun with melted swiss cheese. Someone must have ordered them, because they stayed on the menu, but we never dreamed of eating them, not with the available alternatives.

Cincinnati chili was still in its formative stages, with Empress dominating the market and Skyline and Gold Star not yet on the scene. We would never take a date out for chili anyway: too gauche and too uncertain on the stomach. My personal strategy was to take dates to dinner and the theater. I enjoyed the kind of plays that were capable of attracting a Cincinnati audience, and going to the theater made my dates feel as if I were somehow different, somewhat older and more mature. My restaurant of choice was the dining room at the Carousel, an upscale motel between Roselawn and Reading. (My parents preferred Pompilio's, on Washington Avenue in Newport, a nice family place that was later used as a set in *Rain Man;* it's there that Raymond counts the 246 toothpicks that have fallen to the floor.)

If there were no plays in town at the time, the choices for movie theaters were exceptional. The Valley—just a few blocks in from the Carousel—featured large-screen epics like *Around the World in Eighty Days,* and the theater itself was huge and functional, a vast auditorium where every seat offered an excellent view. My theater of choice, however, was the Albee, a vaudeville palace on Fountain Square with all of the class and style of Radio City, but with fewer balconies. (Sometimes there were problems. I saw *Psycho* at the Albee, and the woman in front of us was so frightened that she wet her pants. When the lights came up, my date and I could not help but see that she had done so, but we each remained decorously silent on the subject.) The Keith's was nice also. Just up from the Gayety Burlesque was one of the country's dedicated Cinerama theatres, where we saw *This is Cinerama, Windjammer,* and other Cinerama films.

I never made it to the Gayety. One of my classmates went there one afternoon (on a school day) and reported on his experience to the rest of us. "The girls were old and floppy," he said, "and the comics were lame." Sample joke: "Hey, is that Dick Brown?" Answer: "It should be. It's been out in the sun all day."

For years the Gayety sat next to the Greater Cincinnati Library, each presumably providing knowledge of different kinds to different clienteles, or to different sides of the same clientele. It disappeared years ago, along with other forms of "adult" entertainment, driven out of Cincinnati by the well-known crusader and now convicted felon, Charles Keating. It left Cincinnati forever, only to be relocated to Newport, Kentucky, just across the bridge.

Newport found its own crusader in a local politician and former Notre Dame quarterback, George Ratterman. The criminals retaliated by drugging George and putting him in bed with a stripper whose name (my memory is shaky here) was either April Flowers or April Showers. George beat the rap and cleaned up Newport, the "adult" entertainment promptly moving to Covington, an adjoining community.

This is a blank part of my experience. The closest I ever got to the "adult" sector of the entertainment economy was the viewing of signs painted on my classmates' backs during a football pep rally. The signs were done in bright blue paint, and they advertised Corky's, the most famous brothel in northern Kentucky. All of the students laughed knowingly and uncontrollably, while the priests laughed sympathetically but ignorantly. My conspiratorial classmates received ten demerits ex post facto when the identity of Corky's was later discovered.

This was a world I knew only through secondhand reports. With my '50 Plymouth ($275 from the used car lot of Schmidlapp Olds) and my dinner and theater strategy, I dated nicer girls and went to nicer places. By then, I was an upperclassman, thinking about college, living a very different life than the life of a sixth grader, but sometimes remembering the strange innocence of those days. It was the time in between, however, that I especially remembered, the time when the girls we had befriended (and who had befriended us) drifted away from our lives and discovered older boys, boys they were ready to call guys and sometimes, even, men.

One incident in particular stood out from the rest. It happened at Swifton Center, the minimall to which Max's later relocated. On the west side of the mall, opposite Woodward High School, was a restaurant and lounge which, for that neighborhood, was modestly upscale. With Crest Hills Country Club to the north and a bowling alley to the northwest, however, this was a long way from first class.

The restaurant had its pretensions. It required jackets of the gentlemen who patronized it, but the loaner jackets which it offered ("Perhaps you could try on one of ours . . .") were straight out of the Moose Lodge, with light pastels warring on the rack with broad plaids.

The pike Big Boy

Swifton Shopping Center. The photo shows normal business activity on a weekend afternoon. The upscale restaurant was just to the right of the pedestrian.

One day when I was walking away from the center, a group of girls from my class were suddenly walking toward me. They were on their way to the restaurant, accompanied by their dates. I immediately noticed four things: their dates looked as if they were forty years old; the girls' faces were layered with heavy makeup, particularly around their eyes and mouths; they were hobbling across the gravelly blacktop parking lot in very high heels; and they were wearing jackets and shawls edged in fur, the latter probably belonging to their mothers.

Our eyes met, and theirs immediately closed. Then, looking down at the ground, they continued to walk toward me. There was a perfunctory mumble of recognition, as if I were a servant or distant, younger relation. I was wearing jeans and a tee shirt, while their dates were all in suits, several of them carrying cigarettes. They looked through me and continued on their way, laughing and joking.

I didn't give it a great deal of thought at the time. I knew that that was the way things were. Girls our age dated boys much older. I think about it now, however, and I think about it often, perhaps because of the inescapable fact that, in the succeeding years, those girls have become middle-aged women. They have married, they have had children; several have divorced, some have remarried, and their children have left them to find their own lives, while they themselves reach out to a past that becomes ever more distant. Now there are reunion pictures, both from our grammar school and from their high school. With the passage of time, their husbands now look the same age as my classmates, except for those who have lost their hair and now look much older. The women wear less makeup. The wraps edged in fur are long gone and with them the three- and four-inch heels. The women are broader in the hips, and the years are visible in their eyes and in the ways in which they stand and carry themselves. Youth is an ideal now, not a failing. Youth is a memory now when they can no longer attract the young but only dream of them. Youth is not a source of embarrassment but a reminder of all that has passed.

When they saw me in that parking lot on that fall afternoon, they wished to part from me forever so that they might find their adulthood. Now they have found it, not in a wider world, but in the world their parents never escaped. It is sad in its way. Women are forbidden to have younger men unless they are rich, no matter what their desire. Unlike my friend Paula, these women gave up their chance when it was presented to them. She chose the young when she could and made them feel young forever.

6

1954

On the Road

In a small town, the only person more prominent than the mayor or sheriff is the funeral director. He doesn't have to be reelected, and he doesn't have to smile. In fact, it's better if he doesn't smile. His job is sympathetic concern, not entertainment.

In our town, the biggest kid was the undertaker's son. He played first base on our Little League all-star team, and everywhere we went he had to bring his birth certificate, proving to the skeptical parents, manager, and coach of the opposing team that he could be six feet tall but only twelve years old.

It was a long journey to the all-star team and the playoffs, so I'll begin at the beginning. Before you could even play, you had to be drafted. Before you could be drafted, you had to try out, but the tryout was an informal free-for-all. My friend and I tried out for the League at Dorl Field, the park adjoining the U.S. Playing Card factory, opposite Dickman's Cafe. All those familiar faces from picture cards—queens, jacks, and kings—were born in that factory, including the little king of spades with the big head riding the bicycle. The field was a few blocks east of the pike and a few blocks south of Waterworks swimming pool and the field below it where the Little League games were actually played.

The tryout park was big, with multiple fields and plenty of open space in which to show off your abilities. Or get lost. Our biggest problem was trying to find the managers so we could work our way into their line of sight, impress them, and entice them to bid on us. There were a lot of people there that day, but not very many who looked official. It was like walking onto a tryout stage when the auditorium was empty or trying to dance in front of a roomful of people, all of whom were turned in the opposite direction. The field was a mix of mass confusion and mass indifference. I was with Donnie Freyer, and, after splitting up for fifteen minutes to make the circuit of the park, we still hadn't seen anyone who looked remotely like a Little League manager.

We were looking for older people with ball caps who might be carrying clipboards or notebooks. Whistles would have been a good sign, too, or maybe a propensity to spit. We did see one guy who looked promising. He was sitting beneath an elm tree, staring across the field. However, when he reached under his leg and pulled out a pint bottle in a brown paper sack rather than a notepad or pencil, we decided to move to the other side of the field.

It took us two hours to find a single prospect. There were only a few minutes left for the tryout, and this was our first and last shot. He was tall, and he was wearing a baseball cap. He was also asleep, sprawled out at the bottom of another elm tree (but on the north side of the field), with his shoulders resting in the exposed roots and the ball cap over his eyes. He was wearing a tattered yellow tee shirt with the faded name of a baseball team written across the front.

Donnie and I got as close to him as we could without being too obvious about it and started to toss a ball back and forth. We were throwing hard, hoping that the sound of the ball hitting the pockets of our gloves might wake him. It took us ten minutes to get him to the point where he was ready to change position and readjust his hat. Eventually, he pushed his hat back, and we saw his bloodshot eyes.

We tried everything. We threw balls up in the air and played outfielder. Then we threw ground balls and played infielder. Donnie squatted and caught my pitches, then I squatted and caught his. We must have done something right because, just before the end of the tryout, the guy stood up and asked us our names. We told him, he wrote them down, and then he walked away.

Then we waited. And waited some more. Months later I found out what happened. The draft occurred in a bar called the Wooden Shoe Cafe up on Montgomery Road, and I was picked by the guy laying under the tree, who was indeed a team manager. This turned out to be a rare bit of luck, because I learned later that the guy had been thrown out of that particular bar and was only allowed back that one day in order to participate in the draft.

He bid on me and got me for eight hundred points, a price no more than a breath away from the bargain basement, but at least he bid on me when no one else did. The team was sponsored by Allis-Chalmers, the tractor people, and the manager's name was Draple. I found out later that his first name was John, but no one ever called him anything but Draple.

Draple was basically a drunk who bounced from job to job but always stayed with baseball. He was always sober at practice and always deadly serious about his team. He had trouble keeping coaches because of his manner, and he regularly reduced his nine- to twelve-year-old players to tears. When a lesson was to be learned, he made you do what you had to do over and over until you did it right. The fact that you might be standing in the middle of the field, humiliated and sobbing uncontrollably, meant nothing to him whatsoever. He taught; you learned. If you quit, he taught someone else.

Parents might be standing by, clutching at handkerchiefs or threatening to sue, but that was immaterial to him. He had nothing to lose and no place else to go. He stared through them from time to time and then turned his attention to their sons, hitting endless balls at their feet or requiring them to perform some maneuver until they performed it correctly. He never cursed or shouted, but he never stopped the lessons until they were learned.

When we made the team, we were issued our uniforms and hats. Some of the boys wore their hats to school for a week or two to show them off. They were a new badge of honor, and the boys

Dorl Field. My tryout site was at the approximate location of the soccer goal on the opposite side of the field.

The Wooden Shoe Cafe. The door left open on a hot, humid day, it has changed very little in forty-six years.

curled the bills over and over, trying to get just the perfect curvature at the sides, that shape that said, "I've had this hat forever, and it fits like a kid glove." I kept mine at home, protecting it.

Our team was respectable and solid but never a contender. The favorite team was the Highlanders. The Highlanders were a social club to which most of the managers belonged, and the club kicked in to sponsor one of the teams. (Draple wasn't a member.) They also had a fishing camp down on the Ohio River, below Terrace Park. We went there once. It was supposed to be an outing or something. When we saw the camp, we were surprised because there was nothing there. It was essentially a shack without any furniture except for a card table and some folding chairs.

Basically, the Highlanders went there to drink and play cards. I didn't see any fishing tackle or boat equipment. The single table was sticky with dried beer, and the ashtrays were overflowing with cigarette and cigar butts. They had a stack of napkins, most of which looked as if they had been used a couple of times and then put back into the stand. There was a picture on each napkin of a guy with a drink in his hand. His head had melted, and smoke was coming from his ears and skeletal eye sockets. Above his head was a balloon with the statement, "JEESUZ YOU MAKE 'EM STRONG."

I played second base for Allis-Chalmers and batted second. Fielding is tough in Little League, because the base paths are short and there's very little margin for error. I was a better batter than a fielder. Sometimes Draple moved me to right or center field, but he never took me out of the lineup.

I was later traded to Schmidlapp Oldsmobile, a better team, though we still had trouble with the Highlanders. The Highlanders had two boys who were big for their age and uncommonly strong. Each could both pitch and catch, and they rotated in those positions. They threw hard, and they caught well—no muffs, no passed balls—and they offered very little opportunity to steal. Each threw overhand rather than sidearm, and each only had one pitch—a blistering, low fastball. One was named Ralph Kaiser, the other Chuck Boucher. The Highlanders also had a pain-in-the-ass leadoff batter who was the shortest kid in the league. His name was Terry Witte, and his strike zone was only a couple of inches high. His head was so small that his batting helmet wobbled back and forth when he walked, but he could run like a deer, despite his short legs. Most of the time, he bunted. He'd bunt no matter what the situation, and, even though you knew it was coming, he was a hard out.

Once on base, he would steal, and he was hard to tag because there was so damned little of him. Their second batter was Petey Shrader. People often compared me with him, since we were both short and played the same position. Petey couldn't hit. All he could do was make contact and run. He couldn't place-hit or pow-er-hit, and his swing was shaky. What Petey had was luck. Since he batted after Terry Witte, the other teams were so concerned about the little leadoff batter stealing that they lost some of their concentration pitching to Petey and tended to forget about him entirely if both he and Terry were on base. Sometimes he would get on base and jump around like a hyperactive rabbit, threatening to steal. He knew that no one but his parents were paying any at-tention to him, and that just made him worse.

I never liked to play the Highlanders, because their battery was all muscle and their scorers were like mosquitoes getting in your eyes and hair. The former were too strong, and the latter were too fast and light. Kaiser and Boucher were also power hitters, so if Terry and Petey didn't get you with chickenshit bunts and steals, Ralph and Chuck would get you with doubles, triples, and home runs.

I never met Ralph's parents, but Chuck's were there all the time. His father was the local league president, the guy who filled out all the forms for the national organization. He liked to put on his old clothes and hose down the field on dusty days. When the water was turned on and the hose gave him little more than a slow dribble he would say, "Jesus, I went harder than this when I got up this morning," and all the kids would laugh.

After the games, we would press our parents to take us out for malts at United Dairy Farmers and miniature golf at Wee Tee in Montgomery. When we won, we wanted the moment to continue, and when we lost, we wanted to do something that would quickly help us to forget.

There were never any girls along, even though the boys were sixth, seventh, and eighth graders and girls were now an increasingly important part of their lives. Little League was a world apart, reserved strictly for the boys and for the boys' parents. The field on which we played was in northeast Norwood. It sat in a dusty valley, below a series of large apartment buildings. The front of the buildings was Cincinnati red brick, but the back was New York tenement with open wooden stairways and wash hanging across the stacks of rectangular porches. The girls from the buildings sometimes watched us play, positioning themselves at the top of the hill in aluminum-and-plastic-strap lawn chairs, while their fathers looked out from their porches, stripped to their tank-top undershirts, cradling quart bottles of beer. We went up to talk to some of the girls once or twice, but for some reason we never connected with them.

That part of Norwood was largely industrial, the only stops on the way between the pike and the field being the White Castle to the west and a bar called Gil's a few blocks closer. The bar had an adjoining grocery, and the owner sold cups of frozen lemonade out of his freezer section. With each cup, you received a wooden spoon in a cellophane case that was used to scrape the crystally juice as it melted. It was a popsicle in a cup, but richer by far in both taste and quantity. Eventually, the owner stopped selling them because he said the kids never had the right amount of money and making change was becoming a pain in the ass.

We liked to go into bars, not for the beer (we were still too young for that) but to steal a glance at the local characters and the mix of language and behavior that shaped their lives. In those days, all of the bars had pinball machines, and some (like their northern Kentucky counterparts) had slot machines. Many of the blue-collar workers from the Fisher Body plant or American

The north Norwood Little League field. The outfield fences and dugouts have been removed.

Gil's Bar and Grocery. It is largely unchanged, both with regard to appearance and briskness of business.

Laundry would cash their checks in bars like Gil's on Friday nights and then blow most of their pay on beer and pinball. There was one guy in particular who was a special subject of our attention, a pinball addict named Gary. The bartender kept a stash of quarters to make change for people like him, and, when Gary came in, he would take most of the rolls that Gil had sequestered. His routine never changed. He would order a glass of beer, take a sip, and then open the rolls of quarters and spread them across the glass cover of the pinball machine. There were so many quarters there that he could barely see the lights, bumpers, and flippers.

For some reason or other that comforted him. He saw his whole night's activity spread out before him. It was a kind of commitment as well. He wouldn't leave until all of the quarters were gone. He grabbed the sides of the machine as if it were an unruly child, and then he tried to bend it to his will, his fingers hitting the flipper buttons wildly as he coaxed the balls with his head and shoulders. Once in awhile, the machine showed TILT and shut down, and, once in awhile, he scored enough points to get a free game, but most of the time he just dropped quarters and passed the hours.

We liked to go into the bars and pony kegs in our uniforms. Dusty uniforms from the city's softball leagues were a constant sight in such places, and we wanted to fit in as best we could. Sometimes there were comments about our rubber-spiked Little League shoes from the men and older boys, but it was a small price to pay to be among them, if only for a few moments.

What we hoped for more than anything else was the chance to play on the league all-star team, since the all-star team entered the play-offs and was able to travel. The ultimate dream was a trip to the finals in Williamsport, Pennsylvania, but our teams never quite managed to get out of Ohio.

In order even to get out of Cincinnati, you had to beat teams from the local leagues. Our rival league—the first we always faced in the playoffs—was from west Norwood, an upstart league whose establishment Chuck Boucher's father had attempted to block.

Unless you got past them, there was no hope of travelling to more distant points, towns with names like Elyria, Urbana, Piqua, Lima, and Washington Court House.

Most people don't know how many teams you have to beat in a one-and-out tournament in order to get to Williamsport. The Super Bowl is easy; Little League is hard. Even then, what awaited you in Williamsport was a cream-your-ass team from Taiwan that played at a level that most of us could barely imagine.

Still, we travelled, though the trips were all low-budget affairs. There was no bus, and there was no caterer. We were driven by our parents in a convoy of station wagons and old sedans, and we ate at Dairy Queens and A & W Root Beer stands. Nevertheless, we were travelling, and those who would never enjoy the opportunity looked at us with yearning and envy.

I didn't make it to the all-star team until my last year, when I was twelve. That year I had done some pitching, with mixed results, but most of the time I played second base. I was picked for the all-star team because of my batting ability, but Petey Shrader was also picked, and he was allowed to start in my position.

Each game was interesting. It started with the presentation of the birth certificates of the taller players. Then we walked out to the first or third base line, put our caps over our hearts, and heard the national anthem played over a shaky PA system. Finally, we saw the mystery pitcher.

For many kids, mastering the simple fundamentals of the game was a challenge. It wasn't as bad as peewee hockey, where even the best players were unable to master the fundamental moves and passes, but it was a challenge, nonetheless. A boy who could move beyond the fundamentals and add something new or different was a rarity. Such boys always seemed to turn up during the play-off tournament.

For most pitchers, the challenge was to consistently throw strikes. It was rare to find a twelve-year-old who could pitch to the batter's weaknesses, and it was impossible in the play-offs since none of the leagues could afford to send out scouts to study the array of teams which comprised our possible set of opponents. The result was a strategy that capitalized on the skills of pitchers who specialized in quirky deliveries or unfamiliar pitches.

It is difficult to throw a curve ball in the distance from a Little League mound to a Little League home plate, and most twelve-year-olds have trouble keeping a knuckleball in the general area of the batter, catcher, and umpire. Instead you saw sinkers, fastballs, and changeups and, in the play-offs, the abovementioned odd deliveries. We saw rubber-armed sidearm pitchers. We saw sidearm pitchers who leaned as they threw and mimicked the motions of fast-pitch softballers. Chuck Boucher's father was always at the ready with threats of formal protest if anything was done that appeared to be less than strictly regulation.

We saw gangly farmboys with size-thirteen shoes which they lifted in the air to disrupt our line of sight before releasing the pitch. We saw pitchers who were abnormally slow or abnormally fast in their release. Anything that might be uncommon, anything that might throw off our timing, anything that might raise questions of legality and distract us from the essentials of the game, we saw.

In league play, you get to know pitchers like that. You see what they're up to, you talk to other people, you compensate for whatever it is they're doing, and you knock them off the mound. In a play-off game, you're seeing them for the first time, and you only have six innings to get used to what they're doing and learn how to deal with it.

Sometimes they had the pitchers warm up off the field, so you didn't see their stuff or their gimmick until the first batter came to the plate. It was great material for later stories because the opposing pitcher's quirks were always exaggerated in the retelling and a lot of drama added as the game was replayed in our imaginations. At the time, however, it was always a cause of concern and sometimes of alarm.

Since the parents were so actively involved in the event there was always the feeling that the ringer pitcher represented a form of cheating, cheating that carried a conspiratorial dimension and implicated the entire town in practices that were low, mean, and unsportsmanlike. That was a good motivator, but, if the opposing pitcher was really good, the demonized opposition could appear to be real demons, and no one wanted to play them.

We thought of ourselves as purer and somehow above such practices. We always gave them Ralph Kaiser or Chuck Boucher—competent, strong fastballers. No tricks, no surprises, just simple ability. That was us. That was our town. Fair play all the way. So what were we doing among these sleazy lowlifes with a secret pitcher bending the rules in an effort to trick and humiliate us?

We counterattacked with Petey Shrader's mother, an overweight woman with a shrill, piercing voice and a proclivity for registering complaints in a clear and distinct fashion and at a high decibel level. At the first sign of any duplicity, she would scream epithets and level charges at the opposing team, its manager, its coach, its parents, its grandstand supporters, its town, its mayor, and its entire benighted section of the great state of Ohio.

This brought boos from the opposition and a rancorous atmosphere that sometimes rattled the opposing pitcher. Boos were food for the soul of Mrs. Shrader. Sartre said that hell is other people. For Mrs. Shrader, heaven was being surrounded by a group of antagonistic people and making them feel as if they were in hell. The louder their screams, the broader her smile, and, no matter how severe the charges were that she had initially levelled, she always seemed able to multiply and escalate them in the face of a violent backlash.

That was good for at least the first half-inning, since she quieted down when our team came to bat, but she could not sustain it forever, as her husband's growing embarrassment combined with the shriller and more focused responses of the opposition to neutralize her effectiveness. By the end of the second inning, we were definitely on our own, and by then a third of the game had been completed. If we wanted to succeed, it was important that our counterattack be swift and decisive.

In my single season on the all-star team, we had defeated the team from the upstart west Norwood league, and then gone on to beat the teams from Hamilton, Xenia, and Bexley. Then we travelled to Bellefontaine to meet our destiny.

Their pitcher was a boy named Roy. There was no mention of a surname. As with most local legends, the given name seemed to be enough. Roy had freckled cheeks, a small face, and long arms. His shoes were scuffed, and his socks were wrinkled, and his stained white uniform looked as if it could use some soap and bleach. He wore his blue cap with white stars down over his eyes, and his facial expressions were hard to read. He threw with the most minimal of windups, the pitches exploding from his hand like rounds from a chamber. There was no time to settle in. The ball was suddenly there, and you had to react.

Ralph Kaiser was pitching for us, and, while his strikes were low and straight and true, so were the swings of Roy's teammates. They teed off on Ralph's sinker pitch, sending hard line drives into left and center fields. We contained them as well as we could, but, by the third inning, the score was 6–0, and all of us—the players, parents, coach, and manager—could feel our season coming to a swift and inevitable close.

In the bottom of the fourth, Chuck and Ralph changed positions and Chuck started pitching tight, hoping to keep their batters away from the plate, swinging for self-protection rather than for the fences or the left-field line. When he hit their shortstop hard, on his forearm, their manager came storming out of the dugout, demanding an end to what he described as brutality and poor sportsmanship. The shortstop was standing on first base, rubbing his arm and snivelling to great effect, and the umpire gave Chuck a warning.

He walked the next batter and served up an easy pitch to the next, who hit it into right-center field for a standup double. The score was now 8–0. The next batter tried to bunt, but the ball popped in the air. Ralph caught it and threw out the guy on second, who by that time was nearly to third base. We breathed a sigh of relief, tried not to look at the scoreboard, and got ready for the next inning.

In the top of the fifth, we scored two runs. Jeff Klug, our towering first baseman, hit a triple with two outs and brought in Bill Barry and Jerry Heinemann. The next batter, Tony Clemmer, bunted, but the catcher fielded the ball, stared down Jeff, and held him at third. Then Chuck Boucher came to the plate and, on a 3–2 count, drove a long fly ball to the left-center field fence which was caught, one-handed, by a kid who looked down in his glove with an expression of deep surprise and sudden exhilaration.

In the bottom of the fifth, Chuck gave up a single run, but in the sixth, with the score 9–2, Roy walked Terry Witte and hit Jimmy Henderson in the leg with a wild pitch. The manager was going to protest but decided to keep quiet in hopes that Roy would be kept in the game, continue to miss the strike zone, and give us a shot.

Ralph Kaiser homered, and the score was 9–5. The parents were jubilant, and the manager momentarily stopped squirming and spitting, but the next batter struck out and the following batter flew out to right field. With two outs, Joe Earlon hit a single to left, and Bob Bisbee walked. The next batter in the lineup was Petey Shrader, and my heart sank. Petey was always too tentative in the clutch, and we were a single out away from being eliminated.

He jumped out of the dugout and started to handle the rosin bag, rubbing it on the handle of his bat. It was almost as if he could feel the thoughts behind him and was trying to escape them. Suddenly, the manager was out as well, standing beside him, with his hand on his shoulder. Petey returned to the dugout, looking as if his mother, father, and dog had just died. The manager wrinkled his lower lip in sympathy, nodded sweetly toward Petey, and then turned to me, telling me to go on out there and pinch-hit.

It was my first time off the bench in the entire series of play-off games, and, while I was pleased, I was also a little hurt that they hadn't turned to me until now. The first pitch was high, and the second was outside. I knew that under the circumstances Roy had no wish to load the bases and that the next pitches would be better.

The third pitch was hard and right at my knees. I swung equally hard and connected, hitting a low line drive directly at the second baseman. The ball struck him in the ankle and caromed toward the shortstop, who by now was in a state of panic. He seized the ball and looked for a play, but it was too late. Everyone was safe, and the bases were full.

Our hearts rose for just a second, until the next batter popped up to the catcher and the game was over. I never bothered to ask whether the second baseman was given an error or I was given a hit. As we packed up our things and headed toward our cars, the manager put his hand on my shoulder and said, "Hold your head up. You kept us going."

On the way back, we stopped at a diner between Vandalia and Dayton. We talked a little about how close we'd come in the last inning and how we'd travelled farther than any all-star team for the last three years. We talked about the rest of the summer and about school in the fall and how we still had another hour and a half to drive before we'd be home.

Joe Earlon was riding in our car, since his dad was dead and his mom had to stay home with his brother and two sisters. He kept looking out the window at the white lights in the farmhouses and the red and yellow neon in the truck stops and service stations dotting the highway. I told him that the single he hit was terrific and that, with one small break, we might have taken the whole thing. "That's right," he said. "That second baseman is sorry he got in the way of your hit. It was just dumb luck. I saw it when it came off your bat. It was a double to right center all the way." Then he sat back, looked out at the lights again, and said that this had been one of the best days of his life.

I never saw him again, but I saw one of his sisters a couple of years later at a high school dance. Her name was Julie, and she was a year younger than her brother. She had light brown hair and dark brown eyes. She said he was fine, that they had moved to the other side of town, that he was at Western Hills ("West High") studying shop, and that their mother was very proud of him. I told her to say hi for me, and she promised that she would. I thought about saying something to her about our play-off game, but that was ancient history, and she had stayed home at the time anyway. Instead, I just smiled, and she smiled back.

I could see something of Joe's expression in hers. He was a good kid. He didn't ask for much, he appreciated what he got, and he always made the most of what he had. I doubt that he ever became rich, but I'm sure that he stayed honest and enjoyed his mother's pride and love. Sometimes I think of him, driving across the farmland in the moonlight, reliving that day in his memory and savoring its better moments. I wish I could see him again. I'd thank him for teaching us all how to find the sweetness in hard days.

7

1955

The Shack

It was never the "caddyshack," just as it was never the "country club" or the "golf course" or the "links." It was the "shack." We went "up to" the shack, which was in Pleasant Ridge, several miles above Norwood. And we never walked to it or took the bus. Too young to drive, some of us rode bikes, but, since that stretch of Montgomery Road was too steep to pump through easily, we were locked into an alternating pattern of riding and walking, punctuated with long bouts of heavy breathing.

The preferred mode of travel for the brave, the stupid, and the foolhardy (which pretty much included all of us) was hitchhiking, the accompanying uncertainty adding a touch of adventure to the trip, particularly on the way back when your Norwood or Cincinnati-bound driver was likely to have stopped at a Kenwood, Silverton, Deer Park, or Pleasant Ridge bar en route. Bonus points for hitchers were given in three categories: when you got to the shack in record time (ten minutes or less), when you were fortunate enough to ride in an open convertible, and when the gods took special mercy on you and you were picked up by an attractive woman driver between the ages of sixteen and twenty-one.

The club still exists; its name was and is Losantiville, an early name for the city of Cincinnati, though it was (obviously) later abandoned. Losantiville was an exclusive club, which is to say it was exclusively Jewish (as other clubs were exclusively not Jewish). The other Jewish club on our side of town was called Crest Hills.

Next to the Swifton Shopping Center, Crest Hills was a decidedly down-market affair compared to Losantiville. Their caddies had a reputation for heavy gambling and preying, financially, on the young and innocent. Losantiville members were occasionally heard to utter the k—— word in connection with the Crest Hills rank and file.

The caddymaster's name was George Nagle, an aging alcoholic with a florid nose, blood-webbed cheeks, and short, oily hair that ran in tight waves across his crown and temples. When he breathed, you could hear all manner of things moving in his nose, throat, and sinus cavities. As the shack was separated from the clubhouse by a stand of pine and hardwoods and linked by a snaking dirt trail, George was seen twice daily carrying his lunch or dinner through the woods from the clubhouse kitchen back to the shack. Late in the day, his steps became less and less certain.

There were three classes of caddies: B caddies, A caddies, and honor caddies. Everyone started out as a B caddy. Honor caddies were those thirty-five individuals receiving the most points for attendance in the previous year. Each time a caddy showed up for work, he received points, with extra points for those days when caddies were likely to be tempted to go elsewhere than to work. Some caddies showed up even when there was little chance of "getting out," just to receive the points. Experienced caddies who were not honor caddies were A caddies, unless they had received bad reviews by their golfers, in which case they could be knocked back down to the lowly status of the B caddy.

Upon the completion of a round the golfer (routinely termed the "gopher" by the caddies, the "member" by the caddymaster) completed an evaluation of the caddy, marking the caddy's yellow ticket "Excellent," "Good," or "Fair." Two Fairs resulted in your prompt demotion to the rank of B caddy. Two more Fairs and you were fired.

Several countermeasures were utilized to forestall such developments. For example, every caddy worth his fee ($1 for nine holes; $2 for eighteen) learned how to watch the members fill out the yellow assignment/evaluation form. Even if you didn't have a clear line of sight at the form, you could at least estimate whether the member was marking the box at the top of the ticket or the one at the bottom. The middle box was more problematic, particularly when there was a lot of shuffling and feinting on the part of the member, but in time the skill could be developed and the body language read.

The tickets were placed in a box just beyond the eighteenth green. In the case of a sure Fair, tickets were retrieved through the slot with the help of sticks and gum or, ideally, gum and bendable lengths of wire. There were occasions when the box was so cluttered with foreign objects lost in the probing for Fair tickets that the caddies were collectively lectured on the practice by the caddymaster. In the case of an irretrievable ticket, the countermove was more desperate: one simply set the box on fire. After three such incidents in a single year, the box was temporarily moved into the clubhouse, a marginally more secure location.

Measures and countermeasures were omnipresent elements in our work. For example, when caddies were done some great wrong (for example, a member informing a guest that tipping was not permitted, just at that moment when the guest was reaching for his wallet), the standard response was to relieve the member of a new golf ball or two, depending on the level of the infraction. This was done in that interval of time between the member's entrance into the locker room and the caddy's return of his bag to the pro shop for storage. Members seeking to avoid such losses counterattacked by carrying all of their golf balls in a cotton bag with drawstrings, tucked into the ball pouch at the base of the golf bag. After the completion of the eighteenth hole, they reached into the pouch, removed the cotton sack with the balls, smiled knowingly at the caddy, and carried their balls into the clubhouse. The resulting countermeasure (particularly if the gloating was extreme) was obvious: caddies stole their head covers, umbrellas, or one or more of their golf clubs.

When the warfare had escalated to an unacceptable level, a meeting was called by the caddymaster, the purpose of which was to recount anecdotes, level charges, and issue threats. The standard countermeasure was a sit down strike by the caddies, who assembled at second base on the overgrown ballfield on the wooded edge of the first hole and ignored the caddymaster's angry cries. Under the right circumstances, a unique mix of sounds resulted. The first was the voice on the pro shop intercom, desperately calling for caddies for impatient members, the second the cries of the caddymaster, and the third a carefully orchestrated hum from the striking caddies, who claimed to be in a state of deep meditation. The sound level of the hum rose in direct proportion to that of the caddymaster's cries.

In between the field and the shack was a horseshoe pit and a crude miniature golf course, carved out of the hard clay and tree roots adjoining the shack. The purpose of these facilities was to keep the caddies on site and otherwise occupied on a slow day. The shack itself contained a Ping-Pong table, the favored pastime site (on which more later). Alternative diversions included the general harassment of B caddies and the setting of time bombs beneath the caddymaster's office. These were short, burning cigarettes with the fuses of cherry bombs or M-8os inserted into the end. The bomber crawled under the shack, installed the bomb directly beneath the floor boards on which the caddymaster's chair rested, and then returned to the porch, where he sat politely and quietly with all of the other caddies, waiting for the explosion and the resultant "JESUS CHRIST!" from the caddymaster. If his chair was knocked over in the process or paper was seen to fly in the air, the bomb was judged to be an especially effective one.

Which brings us to the architecture of the shack itself. The building was approximately four to five hundred square feet in total space, with a Ping-Pong room, the caddymaster's office, and a porch with built-in benches. The caddymaster had an assistant (dubbed his "suck" by the other caddies) whose job it was to sell drinks and snacks to the rest of us. The suck was resented and scorned because it was universally believed that he had free access to soft drinks, popsicles, and such favored items as moon pies and "Nip-Cheese" crackers. In front of the caddymaster's window was an open walkway that was an extension of the porch, and on the caddymaster's desk was the intercom box connected to its opposite in the clubhouse.

The caddymaster first received a request for caddies from the former sucks who had been promoted to jobs in the pro shop. He then decided which caddies to assign to the golfers, following more or less the order in which they had registered for the day. (There was also a "carry-over" list from the prior day, and some caddies came to the shack the day before, particularly on Fridays, so that they could both receive the points and be listed on the carry-over in hopes of getting out early on the course the next day. That materially increased the odds of getting out a second time in the same day, thus increasing the weekend wages.)

When the caddymaster had decided whom to assign to the golfer (working from his three-columned list of B, A, and honor caddies), he called out a number. That caddy then presented himself at the window outside the caddymaster's office. Note that the top caddy would be caddy number one (of the thirty-five honor caddies), but to be caddy number one was automatically to be dubbed one of George's sucks, so an ideal number would be something like eighteen—a number identifying an honor caddy, but one with a number unlikely to call attention to itself. The number thirty-five was, of course, as suspect as the number one, with automatic allegations of a caddymaster fix. Thus, the actual announcement of the number frequently resulted in a succession of catcalls and jokes.

When the caddy presented himself to receive his yellow ticket, his pulse was racing. The eternal hope was that there would be two tickets, not one. Carrying "doubles" meant a double fee. It was also an indication of strength and maturity. There was danger, however, for if one received doubles and a physically superior, senior caddy later received singles (the caddymaster initially overestimating the traffic flow and the supply/demand ratio), there was every likelihood that the smaller caddy receiving doubles would also be receiving, at best, a shove or other expression of anger and outrage from the dominant caddy.

Hence, when the caddymaster was in doubt, he instructed the

caddy not to open his double tickets until he had left the shack. Since leaving the shack meant walking across the porch and through the gauntlet of caddies on either side of it, this was an acquired skill. The pride and pleasure of receiving doubles had to be suppressed and a poker face maintained. At the same time, a who-gives-a-shit attitude and bored expression could be assumed, in the hope that the rows of caddies on the porch might neglect to ask, "Whodjaget? Didjagetdoubles?"

Other scenarios and strategies were also possible. For example, if you received doubles and the golfers were both hackers, the latter news cancelled out the former and kept the dominance relationships in equilibrium. Similarly, a dominant caddy might receive singles but be caddying for the pro, so that some semblance of honor was retained. However, if one received singles and the golfer was a hacker, this information was never revealed, since this was a fate reserved for B caddies of the lowest order. The most dire fate of all was to be assigned to caddy for Nancy Dientz. Nancy Dientz was the worst golfer (without exception and without a close challenger) at Losantiville. She shot in the mid to high eighties (for nine holes), averaged drives of thirty to forty yards (when she made contact with the ball), and spent the majority of her time in the woods and rough.

Because of her proclivity for losing golf balls, she played a brand that was the lowest of the low, ironically named Pinnacles, usually with red or black scuffs and gaping cuts, so that on the rare occasion that she drove the ball into the air and not along the ground, the wind would catch the lips on the surface of the ball and carry it in some unexpected direction. Worst of all, Nancy Dientz added insult to injury by carrying her worthless, lip-scarred balls in one of those damned cotton sacks with the drawstrings, lest a caddy be tempted to steal them.

Enterprising caddies assigned to Nancy Dientz would always keep an extra ball (taken from her bag) in their pockets. Since she forced her caddies to search endlessly for her lost balls, it was useful to have an extra on hand to drop when a reasonable amount of time had elapsed after the initiation of the search. These "found" balls were frequently stepped on after they were dropped, an action taken with two goals in mind: first, to indicate to her how shrewd the caddy was in being able to find a ball that was nearly hidden, and second, to issue a small portion of punishment in return for that which the caddy himself had received in being assigned to such a player.

Whenever a caddy was handed a ticket with the dreaded name "Nancy Dientz" across the top, the caddymaster instructed him to conceal that fact from the caddies on the porch. The purpose of this injunction was to prevent two possible results. In the case of an experienced caddy, whose reaction was likely to be "Shit! I got *Nancy Dientz!*" the caddymaster was seeking to avoid situations in which the resentments of his caddies were needlessly personalized. On the other hand, if the caddy was a green B caddy who responded to the gauntlet, "Gee, I don't know . . . somebody named Nancy Dientz," the resulting guffaws and endless retelling of the event could preoccupy the caddies for a week or longer and instill a collective attitude that could serve to erode whatever remained of positive, shack-clubhouse relations.

The second-worst fate was to caddy doubles but be assigned Irv Feldman and Phil Bryce. Phil Bryce had a hook and Irv Feldman a slice and neither would "take clubs," that is, allow you to walk more or less down the middle of the fairway while they carried a spectrum of possible clubs with them to the site of the ball. The result was that you walked to the left with Phil, then back to the right for Irv, then back to the left for Phil, and then back to the right for Irv. A four- or five-mile walk became, with them, a ten- or twelve-mile death march. Also, each had a large bag—a "trunk"—with an umbrella projecting from the left side, so that, no matter which bag you carried on which shoulder, there was always an umbrella digging into your ribcage and right armpit.

There were additional problems. Irv Feldman and Phil Bryce always played in a foursome with Harry Waxman. (The fourth player varied, the only requirement being a willingness to play with the other three.) Harry hit a straight ball, but he could never get on the green because he always chose too much or too little club and refused to consult the caddy, experience, or common sense. Standing 120 yards from the hole, he would say, "Looks like about a six iron," and then hit the ball forty yards past the green. His successive shots—long, then short, then long, then short— were like the work of a bad artillery officer, trying to bracket and then zero in on the target but somehow always hitting its peripheries.

Irv, Phil, and Harry were also inveterate gamblers, playing match, medal, low ball/low total, bingo/bango/bongo, and every conceivable variation possible. This meant a tally at the end of every hole that was comparable to a Price Waterhouse audit and a reckoning at the end of every nine holes with more possible permutations than a message encrypted by a German Enigma machine.

The golfer of choice was Dick Maxfield, who played in the mid seventies and bought burgers and black cows for his caddies after the first nine holes. An additional perquisite of anyone caddying for Dick was the opportunity to observe his wife (Patricia "Pete" Maxfield), who played braless, had breasts as big as Blondie's, and liked to flash them at the caddies when she bent over to retrieve her ball from the cup.

I personally drew an array of odd and interesting golfers, for example, Dr. Louis Thaler, an eye, ear, nose, and throat specialist who always went out alone. Dr. Thaler was known for the fact that he constantly practiced but never played. Every time he took a shot, he would drop a second ball (sometimes a third and fourth) and try for something better. He was scrupulous about not recording his scores; he was always just practicing. He was skilled enough to be able to play nine in just over two hours, even though he had taken 125-150 strokes along the way.

One of my special favorites was Dr. Barry Levine, a huge dermatologist who wore a noticeable back brace. It projected against the back of his shirt, just above the generous cheeks of his consistently wedgied ass. He never spoke while he was playing, and hence never whined about his back or about his game, though there was an occasional, audible growl when he muffed a drive or missed an easy putt. Dr. Levine smoked Churchill cigars, which he held in the middle of his mouth, securing them in place with his gargantuan lips. The lips folded over the cigar, enveloping it in soft flesh. The caddies' nickname for him was "Buddha."

The Honorable Sheldon Baum was mayor of Cincinnati, a largely ceremonial role in a city with the council-manager form of government, but one which kept him busy enough to reduce his available time for golf. When he played, he played on Thursdays with the doctors. He shot in the low eighties. His game was simple, consistent, and nondescript, unlike his more colorful career as a businessman. His restaurant, the Wheel Cafe (or, usually, "the Wheel") was located just off Fountain Square and featured the finest beer, the finest burgers, and the finest bratwurst in Cincinnati. The white tile floor of the entire restaurant was covered with butcher's sawdust and the waiters were bow-tied, mustachioed creatures from another era.

The pro, Ben Campbell, was nice enough, though he had a bad tendency to turn on his caddy on those days when his game was off. The first time I saw him play, I thought he was a wizard with magic hands and perfect instincts. Losantiville was a long course, with a par of seventy-two. Ben had once shot a sixty-four, and, for a time, I was in awe of him. He played the course nearly every day. The course record, however, was held by the great Byron Nelson, who came for one day, played the unfamiliar course, and shot a sixty-two. I suddenly realized that I had never seen real golf.

The best woman golfer, Mrs. Charles Cohn, was also the city champion. Tall and chunky, she was in her early fifties when I first saw her play, and her swing was poetry. She was the most consistent, smart player I ever saw, and she was always nice to her caddies. She was the one golfer at Losantiville who commanded the caddies' perennial respect. Even Croppleman called her Mrs. Cohn.

John Croppleman ("Crop") was the senior caddy, a high school student who towered above the eleven- and twelve-year-olds. He was also huge, weighing in at no less than 247 pounds. On the wall of the shack, next to the Ping-Pong table, was a gigantic stuffed carp, most of which had rotted away. Crop used to put his finger into its side, picking at it whenever he passed by. Just beneath the carp was a display of faded pictures of the caddies at a picnic. Crop was wearing a grass skirt. His chest was bare, and he had pressed his thumbs into the sides of his nipples to simulate breasts. No one ever commented on the picture in his presence.

The Ping-Pong table was in constant use. The winner of the previous game played the next challenger, so that a good player could continue to play indefinitely. Crop ruled the table. If anyone even dared to walk behind him when he was playing, he would stop the game, turn to the offender, and ask when the "fucking Easter Parade" was going to end.

This was in contrast to Jerry Biting, the second-ranking caddy, a tall and devious type who loved to cheat. When anyone but Crop was playing, Biting would position himself behind them with an empty pop bottle. At crucial points in the game, he would administer a savage goose with the bottle, then sit back and watch the player's game disintegrate as he waited nervously for the next assault.

Biting was Crop's sole challenger, and he was regularly beaten. Crop disapproved of his bullying the younger caddies, that being Crop's job, and he was unusually harsh with Biting as a result. Once Biting actually challenged Crop to a fistfight and landed the first blow. Crop annihilated him, the fight ending with Biting being raised above Crop's head and then thrown to the ground across the twelfth and thirteenth holes of the caddies' miniature golf course.

The closest we ever came to witnessing a murder was the day that Biting got doubles and Crop did not. Crop was assigned to caddy for the pro (a sop from the caddymaster), but it wasn't enough. For the entire day, he paced through the shack, saying, "Fucking *Biting* got doubles! Fucking *Biting* got *doubles! Fucking Biting got doubles!*" Crop was never assigned to Nancy Dientz. That was a given. One day Biting was, and Crop was merciless, asking him endless questions after the completion of the round. It was a show for the younger caddies, a reminder of the absolute positions within the pecking order.

There was only one caddy whom Crop consistently left alone. His name was Timmy Brownson. Everybody left Timmy Brownson alone, including Biting. Once when Timmy was playing Ping-Pong, Biting sat down behind him, holding an empty cream soda bottle. Timmy, who was half Biting's size, turned to him and told him that if he even touched him with that bottle he would take it away from him and kill him with it. Biting got up and skulked away.

Timmy's brother was Barry Brownson, his quintessential opposite. Where Timmy was sullen and troubled, Barry was outgoing and cheerful. Timmy was heavy, Barry thin; Timmy was tousled, Barry neat. Timmy was intelligent but a poor student, while Barry was a grind. In the language of our grammar school magazine, Timmy was Goofus, Barry Gallant. Their mother, Edna, worked as a waitress in the club dining room. She looked old beyond her years. Her husband had died in an industrial accident at the Hilton-Davis chemical plant, and she was left to raise her sons. She worked every weekend and every holiday. Barry commented on it with pride. To Timmy, it was a source of embarrassment and pain.

The actions and events associated with Timmy were legion, but one was legendary. I was in his foursome the day that it happened, and I remember it as if I had lived through it a dozen times. It was blistering hot, ninety-eight degrees at least, with comparable humidity. Lying in the nearly swamplike Ohio Valley, Cincinnati was the recipient of world-class humidity, the kind that hung in your face and on your skin, daring you to move. I remember a single day from my childhood—one day and one alone—in which the summer air was dry and clear. It was always muggy. "Clammy," my father always said. There were dozens of words for it. We were like Eskimos describing snow. Homes that didn't yet have air conditioning were equipped with attic fans which sucked the air through bedroom windows so that people might sleep on long summer nights—fans with sufficient power to pull up the carpets if someone neglected to open the door or windows.

On that day, we were already bathed in sweat from the walk from the shack to the clubhouse. After picking up the golfers' bags from the rack outside the pro shop, we walked to the waiting area, just beneath the eighteenth green, above the pathway to the first tee. We waited forty minutes for the golfers. If they had shown up five minutes later, we would have been entitled to an extra 25¢. Timmy had already collected our tickets and was about to return to the pro shop to time-stamp them when the golfers appeared, fresh from the bar. There were no apologies, not even a comment.

"Jesus," one of them said, "it's hot. Wait here; I'll be back in a second." He went back into the clubhouse, emerging a few minutes later with four towels. "Who wants a towel?" he asked, distributing them to the members. He looked through the caddies as if they were invisible. Timmy dropped his bag and walked into the clubhouse. This was forbidden territory, and everyone, caddy and member alike, knew it. A minute later, he walked out with four additional towels for the caddies, distributing them in a way designed to show his contempt for the member who had thoughtlessly overlooked us. "Here," Timmy said, handing me a towel. "Take it. You'll need it." I felt as if I were about to be arrested.

His golfer told Timmy that he was out of line, but Timmy didn't respond. He didn't speak the entire round. When his golfer prompted him and even prodded him, Timmy stared back at him with a look so filled with loathing that it silenced everyone. We all knew that Timmy was going to get a Fair. That was a dead certainty. It wouldn't be his first. The round was so uncomfortable for everyone that the expressions of the golfers eventually hardened into a resolve for revenge. They had been presented with a peasants' rebellion, and they wanted none of it.

When we finished the ninth hole, they stopped playing, suspending their plans for the back nine. "Give me your ticket," Timmy's golfer said. Timmy retrieved it from his pocket. It was badly crumpled. The member tore it in half and returned the left half to

Timmy to turn in to the caddymaster for his dollar. Standing by the ticket box, he took the right half of the ticket and held it in the air. "I'm going to fill this out later," he said. "I have some comments to make in addition to giving you my rating. I'll see to it that the caddymaster gets my comments directly, so don't get any ideas about setting the ticket box on fire."

The words were dripping with anger and derision. "Give me my bag," the member said. "I want to make sure it gets back to the pro shop in one piece." Timmy removed the strap from his shoulder, dropped the bag, turned, and walked away.

We walked together through the woods in silence. Twenty yards from the shack, I turned to Timmy and told him I was grateful for the towel. I was always glad I said that. When we got to the porch, the caddymaster was waiting for us. He handed us our dollars and called Timmy into his office. He was sputtering mad, and Timmy went silently.

It was nearly an hour before he returned. Even though it was getting to be too late to go out, there were a few golfers anxious to get in a quick nine, and the caddymaster's suck was forced to hand out the tickets while the caddymaster administered his tongue lashing to Timmy. When he raised his voice, everyone on the porch became nervous and apprehensive.

He hadn't hit Timmy. He never did that, but he covered him with drunken abuse. The one thing we could hear over and over was his injunction to Timmy to imitate his brother Barry. "A *good* boy," he said, again and again. "A *good* boy."

We never heard a word of reply from Timmy, who walked out of the office door, turned, and walked across the porch. He looked at all of us briefly, turned to the left, and walked down the steps and away from the shack. We figured he was either going home or going over to the parking lot behind the clubhouse to meet his mother so that he could wait for the bus with her. Neither was true. Timmy was going to the woods adjoining the clubhouse. He was going to the woods because he had decided on the course of action he would follow in return for the humiliation inflicted by the member, an indignity that had later been compounded by the angry sermon from the caddymaster. He was going to set the woods on fire.

Not that he did any serious damage. With that day's humidity level, the woods were more likely to sizzle than to burn. After ten minutes' work, he was able to get some leaves to smolder. Eventually, there was some smoke and the beginnings of a flame. One of the pro shop sucks got an extinguisher from the clubhouse kitchen and put out the fire in a matter of seconds. He confronted Timmy, who remained silent. Then he called the police.

Timmy was taken before a juvenile court judge who subjected him to a twenty-minute harangue on arson, followed by a fifteen-minute description of juvenile hall and what Timmy could expect there if he was ever seen in the judge's court again. His mother and brother stood at his side, his mother hysterical, choking on her tears. Timmy remained mute until the judge started in on his mother, telling her that she should keep a closer watch on her son and informing her that she could be held responsible for her son's actions. She began to shake uncontrollably. At that point, Timmy spoke. He told the judge that the case was about him and not about his mother and that if the judge said anything more to upset his mother he would have to answer to him. He also called him a cowardly bastard.

The fire was big news at the shack, but Timmy's words to the judge were even bigger news. Defenders of his mother among the club membership pressured the caddymaster to let Timmy return, and, when he did, he was immediately dubbed Blowtorch Brownson or, simply, "Torch."

This made the caddymaster apoplectic. For weeks, he could be seen charging out onto the porch or into the Ping-Pong room, yelling, "Don't call him that! Don't call him that!" Timmy himself neither encouraged nor discouraged his followers. He simply went about his business, silent most of the time. His mother was shamed by his actions, and that was a pity, for, as I think about it now, I realize that much of Timmy's anger was caused by his own concern for his mother and the work she was forced to do. That certain members rallied to her support only indicated to Timmy

Losantiville Country Club. Timmy's woods are now replaced by a parking lot; the remodeled caddy shack is at the right rear. The fencing was not necessary (or considered to be so) in the 1950s.

the degree of her dependence on them and the fact that a single action could so jeopardize her family and livelihood. She was saved because they deigned to save her, and that was not, for Timmy, a source of great comfort.

The fact that the action was his was the root cause of his silence, but there was also bitter resentment of his brother, another coward in Timmy's eyes, who would later step right into the role his mother had been forced to assume. "If you let them do it to you," he once said, "they will." The pat response is that sometimes you have no other options, but for Timmy there were always other options. That's what kept him in trouble, and that's what made him something of a hero to the rest of us.

The shack is still there; I saw it last summer on a drive through Pleasant Ridge. I had a few moments to spare, so I pulled off of Montgomery Road and drove by. I stopped, parked the car, and asked a black man in grass-stained overalls about its current use. He told me it was a storage shed for the greenskeeper and seemed unaware that it had ever been used for any other purpose. The porch and steps have been replaced by ramps for lawn mowers, and the windows are now barred. The bottom of the building has been shored up with cinder blocks and the caddymaster's window sealed. The pictures have all been removed from the walls, and the giant, stuffed carp has been buried, probably in a landfill.

I walked out to the first tee, now the tenth. Every few years, they seem to reverse the front and back nine. The caddies are all gone, of course, replaced by electric carts decades ago. I understood the reasons. They were all good reasons. Still, the course looks like an attraction at an amusement park: men and women in pink pants and yellow skirts, riding in toy cars, racing across the grass like children too young to drive.

I don't know what happened to Timmy. I couldn't find his name in the local phone book. His mother's name was gone as well. Barry is an accountant. He keeps the books for the club and leads the local scout group. I saw a picture of him once—in short pants with a sash and a chest full of medals. He has two ramrod-straight kids, one a realtor, the other an appliance salesman. His ex-wife moved out of state years ago.

1956

The Wolfe Pack

His name was Gerald Wolfe, but everyone called him Jerry and spelled it with a *J*. He had been a high school teacher who burned out after fifteen years of constant student and bureaucratic grabass and an unending prospect of paychecks smaller than the janitor's. He woke up one morning, decided to take a right turn in his life, and chose the construction business. He took along the shop teacher, Tom Flaig, and put him in charge of the skilled craftsmen. Then he went fishing with his father Ralph, plied him with beer, and talked him into supervising the laborers, the kids on the summer shift, and the realtors, accountants, and miscellaneous hangers-on. Jerry's dad had always handled the money and the discipline in the family when Jerry was a kid, and Jerry wanted him to handle them both for him again.

Jerry was short and strange with glazed blue eyes and tufts of blond hair standing permanently at attention. His pants rode high, well above his waist, and his shirt pocket was always crowded with pens. Tom Flaig was tall and courtly, with sandy gray hair, pressed chinos, and clean work shoes. He was too shy to be fully comfortable with his job as foreman, and he tried to influence the crew with expressions he considered assertive. For example, whenever his orders were questioned, he reinforced their original intent by adding statements such as, "And that don't mean jack off." "Don't" was not a word that issued easily from Tom Flaig's lips.

Ralph was silver-haired and crotchety. His head was perpetually slumped forward, the creases in his tan neck lined with grit. He carried farmer's handkerchiefs and chewed on toothpicks. While Tom nervously played with his tape measure, tossing it from hand to hand and flicking the end of the blade with his thumb, Ralph would pick up pieces of dry wall and break them into smaller and smaller pieces as he talked and thought.

I worked for Jerry Wolfe for two summers, building tract houses on the northwest side of the city. Jerry was prospering, at least for the moment. His master plan was simple. He would start by building small homes for grateful buyers. When they were ready to move up, Jerry would be ready to move up, too, building larger and larger homes. His former customers would one day find themselves out looking for a new home, and Jerry would be there—standing on a large front porch, before the colonial windows, looking toward the two-car garage and gaslight, ready to shake their hands and stir old memories. He would keep the same clientele for life.

It was a good solid plan, but it never came to fruition. After building three subdivisions of homes and two blocks of four-apartments, Jerry abruptly said, "Piss on it," and moved to Florida. That all came two years later. By then, I was gone as well as Jerry.

The homes on which I worked sold for $15,000, and Jerry personally pulled down $1500 in pure profit on every one of them. He enjoyed the work, but mostly he enjoyed being Jerry. After years of standing in front of a class, trying to make dinosaurs dance, he decided to spend more time sitting back and watching. One day when his wife and kids were on the construction site, one of his kids—an eight-year-old named Kerry—got into a truck, put it in gear, and released the emergency brake. He started rolling down the street toward the main highway. Suddenly everybody panicked. One of the drywall men started yelling, "Jesus Christ, Jerry, your kid's in that truck." His response was one of passive amusement. "No shit," he replied. "The kid doesn't even have a driver's license."

Jerry only had three subjects which consistently interested him: sex, money, and the pouring of new foundations. He talked endlessly and in detail about his wife Doris and their bedroom activities. He described her euphemistically as "wild," but most other men chose words on the darker side of "slut." Henry Kammerer, the hardwood floor man, told Jerry that *nearly everyone* in Cincinnati had seen Doris's ass, but that she was still young enough to go out with those she hadn't yet met. Henry was including himself on the list of have-seens. He told Jerry this in the spirit of concerned friendship, but it didn't seem to phase him. "That right?" he replied, suddenly changing the subject. "Guess where we went for dinner last night? It was expensive as hell, but Doris felt like steak and lobster. We went to that White Horse Tavern out in Covington. She wanted to go to the Yorkshire, in Newport, but whenever she goes there, she gambles too goddamn much, and I wanted to get her home before I was broke and she was asleep."

His financial backers worried about this thing he had for pouring foundations. Once the foundation is in, you're committed. It's a hell of a thing to try to remove. And the moment it's poured, the sections of the precut house come and everything with it. You can't get too far ahead of your crew, and you can never get ahead of your available cash.

Our foundations were never cinder block. Jerry wouldn't tolerate cinder block. Our foundations were always poured. After the excavation was finished and the dozer had moved on to the site next door, Calvin Hoffman and his crew came in and set up the cement forms. They were smooth and heavy, held together by clamps at the top and reinforced with soft steel pins in the middle. After the cement dried, I had the job of knocking off the ends of the pins that projected into the basement. This was an unskilled laborer's job, but it was an easy one. Using a heavy hammer, you struck the pin on one side and then on the other, then back and forth again, until it snapped free. It was a good job for boys; you got to prepare the basement surface for the patching and the Thoroseal coating by systematically breaking things. I always liked the ring of the pins as they caromed off the wall or bounced off the footers. The only skill involved was ensuring that your hammer was heavy enough and that you struck the pins solidly. If you hit them at an angle or with the edge of the hammer, the pins stayed in place, the hammer vibrated into space, and your arm shook as if you had just received an electric shock. It wasn't something you wanted to repeat regularly.

That was the end of the process of preparing the foundation. Jerry only liked the beginning. It was like the sunrise, the start of a new day, or the first date with the new woman in your life. On the days when we poured foundations, you could see a palpable change in Jerry's mood. He'd talk about it first thing in the morning. "When's the truck coming? Let me know when it pulls into the subdivision." A few minutes later, he'd be checking his watch.

The cement was poured into a corner of what would become the foundation and then floated out along the sides of the walls. Calvin and his crew were skilled men working with what looked like crude tools, but everything had to be aligned and everything had to be level. A mistake was catastrophic. Rapidly drying cement is not an easy medium in which to work.

Calvin and his crew were all black, and they worked with a quiet efficiency. They cleaned the flecks of dried cement from their forms with a tool that looked like an icebreaker—a broad blade positioned at the end of a four- or five-foot handle. Once when I used one of their tools for some crude purpose, Calvin took me aside and lectured me on the proper use of implements. "Do you use your razor to cut your bacon?" he asked. I should have said, "Hell, Calvin, I don't even shave yet," but I just said, "No." "Then you don't misuse my tools either," he responded.

When the cement was flowing into the forms, Jerry would stand beside Calvin and move it along. I never saw him happier. Inside the foundation a few days later, life was different. Laborers prepared the way for the skilled workers, filling wheelbarrows full of pea gravel and rolling them along the footers to the distant corners of the dirt floor. I liked to work with pea gravel because it was clean and cool, trapping the subterranean moisture and counteracting the heat of a Cincinnati summer. Sometimes you shoveled. Sometimes you wheeled. Sometimes you did both.

When I did basements, I worked with three other laborers, two of them white and one black. The two white men had three or four teeth between them, and those teeth that they did possess were mostly dark stumps. Their sole subject of conversation was sex, and they managed to stretch the same questions and answers across an entire day. One was named Johnny, the other Bill. They carried pictures of their common-law wives and showed them around as if they were the newest adult postcards from the Left Bank. The women, in housedresses, looked as if they were sixty years old.

The black man's name was also John, but everybody called him Orange, or Big Orange, in honor of his favorite drink. It started one humid afternoon when he wiped off his forehead, looked around at the other workmen, and said, "I do believe I will have another big Orange drink." This became a formulaic expression and led to the bestowal of the nickname. Each time he used it, he accented a different word. "I do believe. . . ." ". . . I will have *another* big Orange drink." He also liked beer, and, from time to time, he'd pick up a quart to drink with his lunch. He kept it in a brown bag and usually sought out someplace private in which to drink it. When Ralph or Tom were off the site, he was a little more open with his beer drinking.

One of Orange's favorite activities was to yell up from the basement to the people working above on the subfloor. His favorite statement was, "Will you please be a little more quiet up there. We're trying to sleep down here." He especially liked to say it when Ralph was in the area, because he knew Ralph always expected the worst, and it was fun to hear him curse and know that he was predictably shaking his head.

Half of the crew was black, but I worked most closely with Calvin and Orange and remember them best. In the fifties, the vast majority of the black community lived downtown, in the west end of the city, while suburban neighborhoods resisted the arrival of black buyers. When black families moved in, signs often appeared nearby saying "This House Not for Sale." Politically, however, the council-manager form of government meant that anyone could be mayor, regardless of race, creed, color, or gender, since the city manager actually ran things. A basically conservative city, Cincinnati had no problems with the installation of Jewish mayors like Sheldon Baum or black mayors like Walt Berry. You could even dodge normal Republican/Democrat designations by declaring yourself a Charterite, that is, a supporter of the city charter. Thus, while racism was institutionalized in jobs and housing, the city had a friendlier public face. Now, of course, it is a predominantly African-American city.

There was also a great deal of joint opposition to bigotry. The Klan, for example, was aggressively attacked. My father-in-law tells stories of Cincinnatians disrupting Klan marches and ripping off hoods to expose the faces beneath. We were told that the acronym KKK stood for "kikes, koons, and katholics" and were encouraged to resist them should they attempt to seek a presence in our city.

Norwood had a single black family, the Lensleys, and my high school had a single black student, though it also had a black teacher, Father Clarence Joseph Rivers. Father Rivers was known for his meticulous attention to the beauties of the English language. He had taught himself to enunciate its many words with absolute precision and encouraged us to do the same, teaching us a series of strange vocal exercises, repeating sounds such as, "Da May Mee Nee, La Bay Da, Pa Fa Da, La Ka Da." He would take us through these exercises, raising his voice with each repetition. Before I heard Father Rivers's voice, I heard Orange's, and his expressions, yells, and calls always seemed more interesting.

Yelling on a construction site could prove embarrassing. One day, the carpenters were roughing in a second-floor bathroom when some potential buyers were walking through the first-floor level. The carpenters were cutting out some studs, and one of them called out, "The pipe has to go through there; take out a couple more RCHs." There was some hammering and then another carpenter said, "Cut out that section there for the vent. No, not there, over to the right, two or three RCHs."

This piqued the curiosity of the potential buyer, who was walking through the house with his wife and mother-in-law. "What's an RCH?" he said to the finish carpenter putting in the kitchen cabinets. "It's a unit of measure," the man answered. "It's a sixteenth of an inch."

"But why do they call it an RCH?" the man asked.

"I'm not sure," the finish carpenter lied.

"You don't know when you're the one explaining the expression?" the man said. "If *you* don't know, who in the hell does?"

"You'd have to ask one of the boys upstairs," the carpenter said.

The man walked over to the stairwell and yelled, "What in the hell is an RCH?"

"It's a Royal Cock Hair, a sixteenth of an inch," a voice answered, whereupon the wife looked at her husband disapprovingly, and the mother-in-law walked out the door.

The top finish carpenter was a man named Zelmer Gibson. Zelmer could install a set of kitchen cabinets, lay in the countertops, hang the doors, and put up the cupboard shelving in a standard house in a day and a half, sometimes less. Jerry Wolfe talked about him in tones of wonder and admiration. Zelmer kept to himself. He worked without a helper and ate his lunch on the floor of one of the back rooms of the house in which he was currently working.

His closest friend on the crew was a painter named Bob Hamer. Bob was a farmer who supplemented his income by working construction. A gentleman with great patience and strength, he could spend a day standing on the rungs of a ladder, giving the boss his best work despite the heat, the humidity, and the temptations to idleness around him.

Zelmer and Bob's only competition was a man named Hank Willis, who did basic erection and roofing. The houses were not prefabs, but they were precut. They came on an open truck and were removed piece by piece. Hank supervised the nailing of the walls to the subfloor and the installation of the A-frames above the walls. When the A-frames were in place, the panels of plywood were installed and trimmed. Hank would have the house under roof by the end of the day in which it was delivered.

The next day, he began work on the roof, first covering it with tarpaper and then installing the shingles. No matter how much heat or how much glare enveloped him, he would work swiftly and accurately. He carried bundles of shingles as if they were Styrofoam, and I never saw him slip or falter, despite the fact that he was sometimes working on high-angled roofs wearing shoes that were slick with mud.

These three men—Zelmer, Bob, and Hank—were the backbone of the operation. The rest of the crew were of a different order, particularly the electricians. The worst was a man named Kenny. His last name was long and crowded with consonants, so he stuck to the first name whenever he could. He was crude and thoughtless. When he was rough wiring a house and had finished drilling holes through the studs, he frequently threw the electric drill on the subfloor rather than setting it down carefully.

His weekends were consumed by his sexual activities, or so he said. He liked to discuss them in detail in an effort to embarrass the foremen. One Monday, I was picking up some empty boxes at the side of a house, and Kenny was sitting in the doorway. When Tom Flaig walked by, Kenny called out to him and told him that he had had three motel dates over the weekend, one Friday night, one Saturday night, and one Sunday night. Each was with a different woman. He told the foreman that he was worried that he might have picked up a social disease.

"What do you mean?" the foreman asked.

Just then Kenny slipped a hammer out from behind his back and put it between his legs, with the end of the handle against his crotch and the head moving up and down between his knees. "I'm not sure," he said. "I think I may have either Hammerhead or Gon-dola." He then laughed uncontrollably as the foreman shook his head and walked away.

I figured that good electricians must have been hard to come by or Jerry Wolfe and Tom Flaig would never have tolerated Kenny. For some reason or other, they never subcontracted the electrical work. The plumbing, on the other hand, was done by two men from a company in Reading. The senior plumber was a man named Dillard who had had a year and a half of college. He told all the young boys to stay in school or they'd risk ending up like him. His partner was a man named Carl whom everyone called Tiny. Tiny was about six feet two and weighed 275 or 280, with very little of it fat except for the pouches around his eyes.

Tiny was the king of the barroom, an expert on weird bets and odd contests and the absolute champion of arm-wrestling. Dillard managed him, and they hustled half the barflies in Groesbeck, Finneytown, and North College Hill.

We used Kammerer's Floors for hardwood flooring (no wall-to-wall in a Wolfe house), and they usually sent out a guy by the name of Roy. Roy was cigarette-thin, with all the wisdom and good looks of the exterminator on *King of the Hill*. He spent the entire day bent over at the waist, nailing planks of hardwood into the subfloor. The planks were loosely positioned, like pieces of a jigsaw puzzle about to fall together of their own accord. He scoot-ed them into position with his foot and then started to nail. He worked with amazing speed and efficiency. I don't know how long he could do that to his body without bad results, but when he worked he worked like a man on a mission.

My least favorite worker on the site, after Kenny, was a man named Harry Kemper. Kemper hung drywall. He was always looking for a young man to assist him. After Kemper hung, taped, and patched the board with drywall mud, his assistant would sand the dried mud until the joints and nail holes were flush with the surrounding surface. The result of this activity would be that the boy was covered in white powder, with grit in his hair, ears, nose, throat, and eyes.

It was too hot, and the boys were too proud to wear any protec-tive covering, so the dusty powder mixed with the perspiration on their bodies to form a thick paste. It was a horrible job, and, as a result, it paid uncommonly well. Harry was always tempting boys to leave school and earn big money instantly. Once in a while, he succeeded, and we looked upon his assistants as semislaves who would be coughing up their lungs by the age of twenty-five.

They moved me around the site, doing various jobs, depending on the need. For a time I painted, receiving a 25¢-an-hour raise for brush-painting some trucks that Jerry had acquired at an auction. For a month and a half one summer, I was given the job of assisting one of the carpenters, a man named Lou Carrino.

Lou was slower than Zelmer, but he was more interesting. His favorite subject of conversation was his wife, Sherry. One day he showed me a picture of her. This came after days of descriptions of her charms and illustrations of the ways in which her charms had affected his life. Just before he showed it to me, he reminded me that the picture had been taken after she lost her figure. I looked at it and had a hard time imagining that the figure had ever been there in the first place, since she was hiding what was clearly a more than ample body behind some loose-fitting sportswear. Her hair looked as if it could have used a good washing. She had a can of beer in her left hand and a cigarette in her right.

"You sort of have to imagine what she looked like," Lou said, and it was clear that he was still able to do so.

Lou was the master of limericks and dirty rhymes, his favorites among the latter usually dealing with the "Three Whores from Baltimore." He could recite verse after verse, especially at a time when I had to focus on something else.

He was the best measurer I ever saw. Much of the time, he was cutting pieces of Masonite with a power saw. He could measure in a matter of moments, turn on the saw, and start cutting rectangles out of the sheets of siding. The rectangles would always fit around the air vents or windows, easily but snugly. This is where I came in. We would each be on parallel ladders, carrying the Masonite up the side of the house, putting it into place, and then nailing it home.

The Masonite was heavy, and there was an immutable law of nature that guaranteed a strong wind in direct proportion to the exposed square footage in your hands. Three quarters of the way up the ladder, just as your footing became less sure and the need for precise coordination became acute, two things occurred. First, the wind picked up and turned the Masonite into a sail. Second, just as you started to wobble and grip the Masonite harder, won-

A Wolfe-built home, with Masonite beneath the gable, the original 1950s shutters, and two decorative guard geese

dering whether it was an enemy or a safety handle, Lou would begin his incantation:

There were three whores from Baltimore, and the bet was which one had the biggest p——y.
And the first one said, 'I've got a c——t as big as the sea;
the ships sail in, the ships sail out and never do touch me.'
And the second one said, 'I've got a c——t as big as the air;
The planes fly in, the planes fly out and never touch a hair.'

And so on.

For a growing fifteen-year-old, the ladder was never high enough to enable me to stand comfortably and nail up the top sections of the Masonite. I had to stretch, and I often had to stand on the not-a-step rung to reach it. By then the wind had died down, but my footing was uncertain and my mind raced between its need to remain conscious of the distance between my butt and the ground and its desire to hear the punch line of the "Three Whores from Baltimore" verse.

Much of the time, my experience was reduced to a set of images: Bill Zepf, a recent graduate of my high school, carrying his box of carpenter's tools across the construction site, an indication of his level of commitment to the job and the irrevocability of his decision to skip college and go to work immediately; the woman at the diner with the neon EAT sign who always referred to our crew as the "Wolfe Pack;" the skilled painter who drew the black wolf silhouettes on the sides of the trucks after I had finished covering them with blue marine paint; the young Kentuckians who bragged about their foresight in opening an account at the Fifth-Third bank a block from the construction site, where they could then cash their Friday checks and make haste to the nearest bar; the accountant in his seersucker suit and bow tie ("Yeah," Lou would say, "Sears made it and a sucker bought it"), our resident intellectual and real-world businessman.

My favorite member of the crew was a man named Little Ralph. This was to distinguish him from Big Ralph, Jerry's father, the foreman, who was never called Big Ralph to his face. Little Ralph's greatest desire in life was to operate heavy equipment. He invariably used a dozer to do a shovel's job, and he never walked across the subdivision if he could drive across in a two-and-a-half-ton pickup truck. Unlike the workmen who prided themselves on their strength (several were able to set thirty-foot steel I-beams into slots in basement walls by lifting them with their shoulders), Little Ralph always looked for something with four wheels and a shovel in front. One afternoon, he took two hours to move a pile of gravel with a tractor because he thought wheelbarrows and shovels were too crude. Big Ralph tolerated this, because Little Ralph was a dedicated worker. He was always the first person on the site and the last off.

Short in stature, Little Ralph had a closely shaved head that was nearly spherical in shape. His nickname for everyone else—tall or short—was "Little Bit." He drove a '56 Pontiac with more things hanging from the rearview mirror than one of the plain pipe racks over at Robert Hall Clothes. Little Ralph actually shopped at Robert Hall for his suits and mouthed their jingles while he worked:

> Let's take the case of Wilbur's dollar. The dollar grew smaller. That made him holler. Why is Wilbur hollering? Because Wilbur's paying for the carpets in the expensive haberdashery rather than for the merchandise. Now at Robert Hall's store with the plain pipe racks, all that you pay for are the clothes . . . (bring up the music) "Low O-o-o-ver-r-rhead, Low O-o-o-ver-r-r-rhead."

I loved that Pontiac, not in itself, but for the freedom that it represented. It took Little Ralph everywhere, and, when he slid behind the wheel, he looked a foot taller and fifty IQ points smarter. When he sat down, he paused, selected the right key from his chain as if it were a fine wine, and gently inserted it into the ignition switch. There were no seatbelts then, but it still took Little Ralph at least thirty seconds to get comfortable and ready to drive. This was his chariot, and he was able to hear the horses even if no one else could.

One day, I asked him if he'd like to go to Lesourdsville sometime. Lesourdsville was a lake north of the city. The water was green and brown and murky in the sunlight, but there was a cement bottom in one area for the swimmers and a beach made of trucked-in sand. When we dove off of the high boards, we felt for the bottom, wondering if there was mud there or cement. It turned out to be cement at the bottom, but there was also mud that had drifted and green bits of plant life. The lake was partially encircled by a set of rides and amusement park games. It was grittier than Coney Island, the amusement park upriver from Cincinnati, but somehow more authentic.

The vast dressing rooms for the pool were filled with wooden, slatted lockers. The smells mixed in the air, and they were all strong: suntan oil, cedar, sweaty clothes, cologne. Real swimmers went to Lesourdsville, not the sunbathers and girl watchers who went to Coney Island. Across the center of the lake was a rope line held up with plastic floats. On one side were the swimmers, on the other fishermen in boats. Sometimes you could feel the fish between your legs and feet as you walked or swam—bluegills and crappies, mostly, though there were rumors of catfish.

"You like Lesourdsville, Little Bit?" Little Ralph said.

"Yes, I do like it," I said. "I like Lesourdsville."

"Well then, we'll just have to go there sometime," he answered.

The most important thing besides Little Ralph's friendship and his Pontiac was his age. I never asked him how old he was, but he must have been almost thirty. He was thirty, and I was fifteen, and we were friends. He was even willing to give up a day of his weekend to go to Lesourdsville with a kid.

Three weeks later, we went and spent the day there—swimming, riding the rides, and walking around the park, eating hamburgers and bratwursts. I drank lemonade, and Little Ralph drank beer. His preference was for Schoenling, especially the Little Kings in the green bottles. We sat on the picnic tables back behind the sand beach and talked philosophically about lakes and summer days and the building trades. He was long on experience and short on opinions. He talked about how things worked and how useful they could be. We went home in the early evening, not because Little Ralph was bored or had a late date, but rather because it was a Sunday and he liked to get up early for work the next day. I remember driving along the highway in that Pontiac, wishing we'd never have to stop. The windows were all open, and the warm air was blowing over our arms and faces as the sun set.

When he dropped me off, he asked me if I had had a good time. I said I did, and he nodded OK. It was as if he had discharged a duty, taken the kid for a ride to Lesourdsville Lake. Weeks later, he would sometimes mention the day that we went to the lake, knowing that it had been a big deal to me.

He never talked about friends or girls or any particular activities he enjoyed. He just sort of worked and ate and slept and drove that Pontiac and tried to oblige people who took an interest in him. There was a sweetness about him that I still remember. He liked machines, and he liked to operate them. He liked people, though he didn't have much to say to them. Mostly he liked the sounds and smells of engines and the feel of keys and steering wheels and handlebars. He never minded being called Little Ralph.

9

1957

The Way Things Are

I remember this Sherwood Anderson story we had to read in college about a kid who finds out that the world isn't as simple and pure as he once thought it was. He idolizes this athlete—I think the guy was actually a jockey—until he sees him with a woman to whom the guy is not married but in whom he is, shall we say, very interested. I've been trying to remember how the woman was described. The teacher was too young to call her "painted" or "loose," but the school was too conservative to tolerate anything much stronger. Anyway, the story was about innocence and about what's really happening on the other side of bedroom walls and doors.

The story was set in a small town in New York, but what happened to me occurred in a large town in Ohio, though it wasn't as lively (or as common) as a sports figure groping a hooker. It happened to me at the Hamilton County Courthouse. Actually, several things happened, though there was a common thread.

I was there working a summer job, helping the lawyers examine real estate titles, which meant going from office to office to see whether or not there were any liens, judgments, or special assessments against the property in question of which the potential buyer (or potential mortgagee) should be aware.

The job was light on theory and heavy on detail and required me to go from room to room and desk to desk checking files, looking at books, and asking attendants to pull cards. This was my first introduction to county government, and the primary lesson learned was that no one in the courthouse was interested in doing his or her job. Nor were they much interested in leaving their desks, since the halls of the courthouse were not air-conditioned. Each of them filled his or her day in a different way. The engineers who put the drawings in the plat books, for example, were all readers. Usually they read the newspaper. Sometimes they read magazines. From time to time, they read novels. These would be pornographic novels, of course—what they called "entertaining" novels, not "improving" novels.

The engineers' assistant, a sixty-five- or seventy-year-old alcoholic named Johnny, was one of the few employees who left the courthouse in midmorning or midafternoon. Johnny shuttled between the courthouse and a bar across the street, on the corner of Ninth and Sycamore. The bar was called Jerry's. When Johnny was at the courthouse, he spent his time smoking cigarettes and blinking hard to try to keep his eyes open. His eyes were mostly green, but with yellow edges and bright red accents. Whenever anyone new came into his work area to ask him a question, he showed them his prize possession: a brass ashtray with a raised carving of a short man in a morning suit standing next to a tall woman in a bridal gown. A barfly's bas-relief. When you turned the ashtray over, you could see that the man's hand was under the woman's dress, giving her a prehoneymoon goose. He showed this object to anyone who would look at it, expecting their eyes to open, their mouths to fall, and their lips to form multisyllabic words, a reaction approximating that of Napoleon's soldiers when they found the Rosetta stone. His question was always the same: "I betcha never saw anything like that before, didja?"

The women who handled the cards listing special assessments for streetlights, new curbs, and storm sewers, or other repairs were all inveterate shoppers. They shopped every day on their lunch hour, taking every second of the available sixty minutes. Sometimes they shopped for clothing, sometimes for household utensils, sometimes for "notions," and sometimes they shopped for food. They never carried less than one full shopping bag home every evening, and they started to get ready to go at ten minutes before 4:00. By 3:55, their coats and gloves were on. By 3:57, they were leaning forward in their chairs. When the minute hand crossed the twelve at four o'clock, they were gone. Any requests for help after 3:50 were viewed as an imposition. Any requests for help after 3:55 were viewed as an affront. They never stopped thinking and talking; they just didn't think about the assessment cards.

The women handling the tax books were altogether different. Each of them hummed incessantly, even when she was stamping PAID next to the individual entries in the large red books which were treated as their personal property and private domain. They had developed the capacity to read a printed list and stamp the tax books next to the right names and plat numbers without any intervening mental activity. This was the one office in which I was unable to work for more than a minute or two at a time. The humming (all of different notes and all at different decibel levels) had me jumping out of my skin from the second I entered the room until the time I left it. It was like an insect house in which there were millions of invisible creatures, all determined to drive interlopers mad.

When I couldn't bear it anymore, I went outside to the tobacconist's stand. The stand, which also carried candy, was run by a blind man named Bill. He knew everyone by the sound of his or her voice. When a stranger came and gave him a bill larger than a dollar, Bill asked someone he knew to verify it for him. Whenever he asked me, I felt a small rush of pride. Bill's eyes were a milky blue. Behind him, filling a small space beneath his legs, was his guide dog, a magnificent German shepherd that never left his side.

At Christmastime, we always brought presents from the law firm to the workers in the courthouse. Greasing the skids. The gifts varied from pint bottles of J. T. S. Brown to $5 and $10 bills in wallet envelopes. I always took something to Bill, even though he wasn't a county employee.

The recorder's office, on the second floor, was filled with fishermen, most of them fat. They had world-class asses, all spreading

The Hamilton County Courthouse

over their raised chairs like lumps of dough on a row of Tootsie Roll Pops. Think of a Dickensian counting house where all of the workers are shaped like Bib the Michelin Man, or a fifties' soda fountain where Poppin' Fresh and his Pillsbury retinue had stopped in for a midday snack. The first lesson the recorder's office clerks inculcated was that there was no good or even tolerable fishing within three hundred miles of the Hamilton County Courthouse. Whenever anyone bragged about his weekend catch, he was immediately asked, "How far did you have to go?" The nearest place that would be considered borderline acceptable was the area of northern Michigan above Houghton Lake.

The head of the office was a man named Harold Cofritz. He had freckles and wore bow ties. He also had the biggest ass of any-

one on the staff and some of the best fishing stories. One of his assistants got in an argument with him one day and started cursing
him in private. I remember the guy saying, "Look at that fat son of
a bitch. That fucking Cofritz. That son of a bitch. I'd like to have
his pants full of *nickles.*"

The books in the recorder's office were huge, but long on fact
and short on plot—an endless set of jaundice yellow copies of
deeds and mortgages, with the cancellations of mortgages indicated by rubber stamps in the books' margins. The files in the sheriff's
office were much more interesting, and so were the people who
tended them. Consisting of endless records of suits, the entree into
the larger files was the judgment docket, a ponderous list of simple, proper names.

One of our running games was to try to find the most outra-
geous, but real, name. The all-time winner: Teaser, Peter. The
judgment docket was managed by two individuals. The first was a
thirty-second-degree Mason named Hendricks, who was always
arrayed in rings, cufflinks, and tie tacks consisting of miniature
scimitars with encrusted jewels. He spent most of his time putting
distance between himself and his supervisor, a man named Teddy
Freyer.

In addition to his putative job for the county sheriff, Teddy
managed two other operations. The first was a fruitcake business
which he ran during the fall and winter months. The proceeds
from those sales funded his annual vacation trips to Florida. Upon
his return from that trip every year, we received accounts of the
trip's highlights. One that I remember in particular concerned his
wife's being overcome with a case of flatulence and revealing her
condition audibly on a crowded elevator. Teddy then tried to do
the chivalrous thing by pretending that he had unconsciously
made the sound with his mouth. For the rest of the elevator ride,
he popped air through his lips as he stared into space. The other
passengers, according to Teddy, were completely fooled.

Teddy's other job was to operate—within the office of the
Hamilton County sheriff—a book. He worked the judgment
docket for the first hour or so but started taking bets in earnest in

the mid to late morning. By the early afternoon, his work for the sheriff was finished; he then spent all of his time hunched over an open drawer in his desk, taking down the names of clients, the names of horses, and the dollar amounts of his clients' bets.

While he stopped short of installing a betting window in his office, he made little effort to conceal what he was doing. This made Hendricks (who was the nervous type) very uneasy. Whenever we asked him what Teddy was doing, he gave us his Sergeant Schultz "I know *nossing*" shrug.

Teddy's lawyer, a man named Buttafacio, asked me to witness his will, which I did. After Teddy's death, I was due a small fee from the estate, which I never got. The lawyer filed a form attesting to the fact that he was unable to find me, which was, in a sense, true, since he was not willing to look up my name in the phone book and give me a call.

That was a small infraction compared with other things that I saw. I lost what little faith I had in the law when I sat in courtrooms during my spare time. The first thing you learn is that lawyers spend most of their time filing papers. They also invest a great deal of energy avoiding difficult judges, but most of their time is spent pushing the paper. Normal days in court consist of a set of people standing around a table shuffling paper at one another—judges, lawyers, bailiffs, whatever. The principal concern is the paper, not the law.

When there are actual court cases, they are not of the sort that occupied Perry Mason. I sat through one actual murder trial—a juicy case in which a woman named Rita Klumpf murdered her lover's wife and burned her body on the shores of a remote fishing lake (one too close to Cincinnati, however, to merit the approval of the men in the recorder's office). In the time between the murder and the cremation, she carried the victim's body around in the trunk of her car while she gave sewing lessons to clients.

The defense attorney was William F(oster) Hoskins, nicknamed Fos Hoskins. He was reputed to be the top criminal attorney in Cincinnati, and his success record justified the title. He would take only two forms of payment: real estate and cash. I was astounded at the shoddy tricks he employed in the courtroom—brandishing a potentially loaded gun, for example, to grab the jury's attention. Deservedly reprimanded by the judge, he demonstrated that the gun had been unloaded and then went right back to work without missing a beat.

In action, he looked like a cross between Perry Mason's slower brother and Bozo the Clown. His physical appearance brought the word "unctuous" to most peoples' lips, except for the lips of most of his clients, who would have had trouble reading the word, much less spelling it or using it in a complete sentence. I once saw him successfully defend a man accused of stabbing a Vine Street "business acquaintance" by pointing to some technicalities in the law and minor problems with the chain of evidence. The defendant had a rap sheet as long as Fos's list of bank accounts, and, if he wasn't guilty of that stabbing, he must have been guilty of something, for the company he kept would have deterred a battalion of marines. In the hallway, after the trial was over, the acquitted man was bragging to his friends about his choice of lawyers. "All you need to hire Fos is one thousand dollars cash money. If you've got the money, you haven't got any other problems." Since this was 1957, a thousand dollars cash money was not an insignificant sum, particularly for a case such as the defendant's, which lasted approximately twenty-two minutes.

The second-best defense attorney in town was a man named Eugene Wells, a tall, meticulously dressed man, who wore dark green suits and had slick, neatly combed hair. He spoke like an angel and reasoned like an eighteenth-century philosopher. I always vowed that if I were ever so unfortunate as to be arrested, this was the man I would call for help.

On a succession of late summer days, I watched him defend a man accused of fraud. The case was simple. The evidence was simple. The facts were simple. The law was simple. The man was absolutely and completely innocent. He had invited a number of individuals to participate in a land scheme that was very high risk but crystal clear in its nature. At first, the money flowed like the Nile, and his investors were at his feet, kissing him toe by toe.

When the flow slowed to a trickle, they were at his throat, demanding his death, a death that was to be preceded by a series of exquisite tortures, each applied in protracted, baroque ways.

Eugene Wells presented the defendant's case. His client was not Albert Schweitzer, obviously, but what he did was absolutely legal, and each of his investors knew that it was legal. They also knew that the investment was chancy, and each and every one of them stayed on board while the investment was successful. The moment it turned south, they turned on him. Wells's conclusion: that's life among the rich and financially adventurous. Their complaint against his client was appalling, absurd on its face, and another example of their own palpable greed.

I sat back against the dark oak bench in the visitors' section. There were no more than a half-dozen people there, listening and observing. Some had come in off the street for a nap. Some were soaking up the air conditioning. That was a pity, I thought, because more should have been there to see this master attorney at work. I wished his words could have been recorded, his expositions and logic studied. Unfortunately, he lost, and his client was sentenced to jail. Why? Because the prosecutor presented a case that could only be described as totally and completely unconscionable.

His attack was *ad hominem,* with no concern for the law or the defendant's rights. He portrayed the defendant as "a man with thousand-dollar bills coming out of his suit." The jury, which was essentially poor and uncomprehending, was urged to think of their own economic condition and compare it with the defendant's. The fact that the complainants knew precisely what they were getting into was glossed over completely. The case became an occasion for a series of diatribes designed to incite class warfare, and the jury bought every last word of it.

What was worse, the judge sat there and said nothing, as if a purely emotional appeal without regard to any relevant points of law were standard operating procedure in his courtroom. My own response was a feeling of instant helplessness—if this disgraceful demagogue could get someone convicted, regardless of the facts of the case and, clearly, the law, and if the judicial moron in the black robe was prepared to go along with it, we were all vulnerable.

Mostly I felt bad for Wells, whose work and performance had been superb. He seemed in better spirits than I would have been, probably because he felt he could win when the case was appealed to a judge with a functioning central nervous system.

A more bittersweet case—one tried no more than a few weeks later—also marked the end of the summer of 1957 for me. This case concerned the Beechmont drag strip, the center of many of our young lives. A group of "concerned neighbors" had brought suit to have the drag strip closed on the grounds that the noise levels coming from the cars were obnoxious and unacceptable.

The races, of course, occurred only on dry weekends during the summer months, so we're talking about two or three dozen days out of 365. The strip was located in a section of town near some scrub pine and shanties that sat above a heavily travelled viaduct and some warehouse property. I had never even seen homes near the strip, but there must have been some somewhere. There was also an airport nearby, but the concerned neighbors seemed to be able to handle the daily noise from the planes better than the occasional noise from the kids' hot rods.

Whether or not the noise of the cars was music to some ears was not explored by the participating attorneys. It *was*, as you might expect, music to ours. The click of carburetor linkage atop an Edelbrock manifold with six Holley carbs or the throaty pulse of an open lake pipe were harmless examples of freedom and power, sounds capable of keeping teenagers off the streets and out of trouble, inviting them to congregate in a drug- and alcohol-free setting where the focus fell on questions of skill and engineering rather than upon the infinite variety of possible acts of teenage mischief which were regularly discussed in, for example, high schools. Ultimately, every drag race was a race against the clock, a few moments in time that were pure in their purpose and compelling in their reality, something that was rarely experienced in what remained of the participants' daily lives.

The plaintiffs, of course, were shrill and fussy, the sort with too much time on their hands and an eagerness to impose the results of their personal need for activity and self-validation on their fellow man. They were the kind who were unable to lead a scout troop or coach a Little League team and were too far down the Nietzschean food chain to run for school board.

There was no one else in the courtroom but the principals and me, and therein was the lesson. The kids at the Beechmont drag strip understood cars in all of their complexity. What they didn't understand was the law and the ways in which the law could be used to take away their summer afternoons without them even saying a word or casting a vote. Nowadays they would probably be at the battlements, countersuing, mugging for the press, standing behind their lawyers as they pummeled the opposition with invective and sweet reason. Not then. They didn't do that kind of thing in 1957. When the strip was shut down, it simply ceased to be. Case closed.

We still had our memories, however. The lawyers for the concerned neighbors had not yet discovered a way to erase or confiscate them. Many of the memories were part of the institution itself—seeing the legends on a local track: the Arfons brothers' Green Monster, a dragster with an airplane engine, hot at the time at 149 mph in a quarter mile; Tommy Ivo's dual Buick-engined rail job that had been featured in countless beach movies; and a visit from the master himself, Big Daddy: Don Garlits and his car, the Swamp Rat.

Some of the memories were more personal, memories of my own modest attempts on the strip, for example, with my aged Plymouth classified F/S, the lowest possible category for an unmodified machine; memories of great races and great cars, the smell of an engine burning alcohol, the sight of parachutes springing open as dragsters hit the finish line and starters jumping into the air with the wave of their flags.

Among them my fondest memory was of a single June afternoon. I must tell you that the memory is real, the story true.

Events that seem fabricated because of the purity of the narrative and clarity of the point do sometimes occur. We remember them best and spend our lives trying to convince others of their reality because of those characteristics. This was one such event.

It happened on a Sunday. The sky was overcast, the strip and pits dry, the cars fast. A low-slung, customized, black '55 Corvette was racing a '32 Ford coupe with a '57 Chrysler engine. The coupe was annihilated, destroyed. It was no more than two-thirds of the way to the line when the Corvette was crossing it.

Then things got interesting. The protocol at the completion of a race was for the cars to come back to the pits on the return strip, a dirt road that ran beside the asphalt-paved, parallel drag strips. The Corvette, however, turned in the traps and returned on the drag strip itself, an act of high arrogance calculated to enrage the observers and the other drivers.

In those days, there were no staging lights between the two drag strips. Instead, a starter—often a woman—stood between the two cars. She pointed to each with her starter flags. Having alerted them, she quickly raised one of the flags, flipping it over her shoulder as a signal to begin the race. This was often accompanied by a leap in the air as the tires squealed and the engines howled.

When the Corvette returned on the strip itself, the starter stepped over onto the strip and waved her flags at the driver, indicating to him that he should get off of the asphalt and drive on the dirt road. He continued on, coming right toward her until she was forced to leap out of his way. This compounded his breach of protocol and resulted in loud jeers and a number of angry threats.

Turning around at the edge of the asphalt, he drove back onto the strip and positioned himself for another race. This constituted a third example of arrogance and disdain, since there were other cars waiting to race and he was expected to wait for his turn. Instead, he went ahead of all of the other cars and sat at the starter line, revving his engine, his car shuddering, his exhaust pipes crackling. His message was clear: I will leave only when I am defeated. The corollary was also clear; given his performance in the previous race, it was highly unlikely that anyone would be able to beat him. Unless he was physically confronted, perhaps even attacked, he would continue to flaunt the rules and humiliate the other drivers. If he *were* attacked, it would constitute an acknowledgment of the fact that he couldn't be defeated on the strip.

Within the quasi-chivalric rules and protocols of drag racing, this was an act of some moment, a challenge that both electrified and disturbed the crowd. No one was prepared to see this individual preen and posture, particularly after he had willfully breached the rules and physically threatened the woman serving as starter. On the other hand, any unsuccessful challenge to his dominance would further feed his ego and reinforce his behavior.

After a five-minute standoff, a car emerged from the pits—a modified Ford that had frequently won in its class. The cars waiting in line behind the strips backed out and made room for the Ford to drive through the gate and challenge the Corvette. The starter took her place between the cars, still a little shaken but desperately anxious to see the Corvette beaten.

The Ford was promptly destroyed. It was no more than halfway down the strip when the Corvette crossed the line. Moreover, the Corvette returned on the asphalt strip again, this time driving at a far higher rate of speed than before. This time, the starter did not attempt to stand in his way. The driver of the Corvette stopped, turned aggressively in a cloud of grit and dust, and positioned himself at the starter line a second time. Waiting.

By now the crowd was in a state of actual rage, and violence was becoming a more likely possibility. The announcer called for peace and patience, but the crowd was restive. This seemed only to encourage the driver of the Corvette, who revved his engine in time with the shouts of the crowd. Finally, in a state of some desperation, the announcer implored the drivers in the pits, asking if there was anyone who could challenge the Corvette.

For a moment there was silence, a silence heavy with disappointment and fear. The silence was replaced by an urgent, steady hum of questions and complaints. Then, suddenly, something happened. I hasten to add again that it really did occur. It was the stuff of romance and faëry, but it was real. It happened just as I will describe it.

There was a sound in the back of the pits, and the crowd immediately fell silent. The sound was that of an engine starting and then revving. With each rev came the unmistakable blower whine that one read about but seldom heard. "Blower" was the street name for a part whose technical name was a supercharger, a huge barrel-shaped device installed between the carburetor system and the engine proper. A supercharger was beyond the budget of any person of our acquaintance. A supercharger cost more than an hour of Fos Hoskins's time. Holes were cut in the hoods of cars so that superchargers could be accommodated. They sat there, breaking the line of the car, announcing their presence and their authority. This one, it turned out, was not visible, because the entire front of the car had been reshaped, the hood raised, to avoid any potential wind resistance. This muted the sound of the whine, making it even more ominous.

As the car left the pits, there was a dust cloud surrounding it and signalling its movement. Only when it approached the gate at the back of the strip could it be seen fully. It was a '57 Chevy, a two-door sedan, painted in grayish red primer. The body of the car was drilled with as many holes as the fenders could sustain without collapsing, thus reducing its weight to an exceptional degree. As it moved, there were puffs of dust from the holes nearest the engine, as if it were ready to explode on the spot.

The message which the car carried was clear. It served one purpose and one purpose alone. It would never be driven on the street. It could never be driven on the street. It represented an investment of thousands and thousands of dollars, all directed to a single, simple end: to travel one quarter of a mile along a simple asphalt strip in the shortest amount of time possible.

When cars drive onto the strip, it is common for them to accelerate rapidly, clearing the dust from their tires in a sudden squeal so that their traction is enhanced during the actual race. Thus, drivers would pull onto the strip, squeal forward aggressively, hit the brake pedal hard, and then shift into reverse and pull back to

the starting line. Some cars accelerated in each direction, an especially aggressive act, designed to make a point with even greater
insistence.

However, when the primered Chevy drove onto the asphalt it
did so slowly and deliberately. There was no acceleration, no
squeal of the tires. The car simply pulled up beside the Corvette,
like a butcher approaching a carcass.

The starter looked like a woman transfigured. Her gait was
different, her eyes were bright. She strode between the cars, carrying her flags. The Corvette was revving hard; the primered Chevy
quietly idling. When the flag came up, it was almost as if it had
been attached to the Chevy by some invisible, all-powerful wire.
She snapped her arm, and the Chevy leaped into the air, dust exploding through its fenders. The sound of its engine was a hellish
scream, a single piercing cry of otherworldly power and pain.

There was no vibration. There was no uncertainty. The Chevy's
traction masters locked its springs and sent it on its way without a
whisper of challenge. Suddenly one knew why car manufacturers
gave their creations the names of big cats. At the moment of perfect readiness, the car leapt forward like a huntress, its eye, mind,
heart, muscle, and marrow fixed on its kill.

It seemed to land long after it crossed the line, the Corvette far
behind it, still surrounded by the Chevy's dust and moving like a
fat, ungainly animal through the thick air of a hot, open field.
Most of all it looked confused, as if it had seen visions beyond its
ken. When it finally crossed the line, like a forgotten runner in a
marathon that seemed to end hours before, it drove off into the
pits and out of the park.

There was a collective sigh as the impact of the event sunk in,
then a desire to bask in the warmth, reliving it a second time and
then a third. The event was holy. We knew it was holy, because no
one approached the gray red primer Chevy in the back of the pits.
It was an unapproachable god that had risen up to silence its people's enemy and now returned to its isolation and its quiet.

We never saw it again. Its existence passed into local legend,
and those who were not there to see it regretted the fact forever.

There were other moments—like the night that a phantom Oldsmobile with Kentucky plates and a padlock on its hood blew Little John Rennert's coupe away on a lonely stretch of Montgomery Road just beyond Kenwood, or the time that Jerry Handleman slipped a big Chevy V-8 engine under the hood of his sleeper '51 sedan and befuddled the gamblers who raced after midnight on the expressway just below the National Distillery—but there was nothing like this and to see it, I must tell you, was to see justice itself, sweet and rare and twice as big.

10

1958

Skating on the Rim of Hell

It wasn't the only time that I tested the divine odds, but this time I did it without a safety net. And the other time, the time before, I was smart enough to check with a priest first—Father Francis Stottlemaier, my sophomore history teacher. My high school was run by the Marianists, but either there weren't enough Marianists to go around or someone was looking for work, since we also had a group of diocesan priests (assistant pastors and such) who taught us. Father Francis Stottlemaier was one of those.

Maybe he liked the idea of working with the Marianists, because every Marianist goes to heaven. That, at least, is what we were told. When I checked further, I found out that someone had stretched things a little. I found a quote attributed to a holy man who, it seems, was impressed with the Marianists. He especially liked the idea of an order that was dedicated to Mary, and he commented, in passing, that everyone of them should go to heaven. This transmuted into the notion that everyone of them *would* go to heaven. And perhaps they would. Perhaps they did. Anyway, it looked good on a recruiting poster, and a number of my classmates hedged their bets by joining up.

If you had known my classmates, you would know why they were looking for a sure thing. Not that they had led lives of constant sin and complete debauchery. Rather, they had grown up believing that nearly every act of which mankind is capable is proba-

bly an act of mortal sin and deep debauchery. They believed it because that's what they were told.

I don't know what Father Stottlemaier believed, but I do know
that he and I always got along. The first day of school, he told us
we should do whatever he said and, thus, stay out of trouble. If we
didn't do what he said, the assumption was, he would hurt us in a
thousand unspeakable ways. If we did, "we would all get along." I
gave him a wide berth, and we got along, so much so that after he
left our high school and got a job at the chancery I felt comfortable enough to give him a call.

A job at the chancery was a big deal. We were always told that
anyone with a job at the chancery was on the fast track to being
made a bishop. (I always liked that word "made." Maybe that's
where the mafia got it. They all had bishops back in Sicily.) Why
were the odds good that Father Stottlemaier would get the big
pointy hat with the ribbons? Because the Vatican dealt with the
chancery all the time, and a smart young guy who played his cards
right would become known in all the right circles. They said it a
little more gently than that, but that was the bottom line.

This struck me as an odd idea. Not that I figured that bishops
were somehow holier than everyone else, or smarter, but it seemed
that the job was important enough that more would go into filling
it than some cardinal's trying to remember who the telephone op-
erator was at the other end when he had dealings with the Arch-
diocese of Cincinnati.

POPE: Cardinal, we need to fill that Cincinnati slot.

CARDINAL: Right, your Holiness.

POPE: Somebody good this time.

CARDINAL: Absolutely, your Holiness.

POPE: So who have we got?

CARDINAL: Well, there's that guy from Gethsemane Monastery, that Thomas Merton guy.

CARDINAL: That's Kentucky. I don't want any problems with
the locals. Who else?

CARDINAL: There's that theologian at Xavier University.

POPE: A Jesuit? You've got to be kidding me.

CARDINAL: But your Holiness, I'm a Jesuit.

POPE: Don't remind me.

CARDINAL: Well, there is that guy at the Cincinnati Chancery. You remember, that young guy.

POPE: The one who redesigned their letterhead?

CARDINAL: That's the one.

POPE: Whenever you call, he's there.

CARDINAL: He is. He's always there.

POPE: Well what are we waiting for?

CARDINAL: He just made monsignor last year, your Holiness.

POPE: (musing) In my day it took years to make monsignor. Then you'd sit around, hoping to be made an auxiliary bishop. Sometimes the call never came. Oh well, that was then, this is now. Call him up. Tell him he needs to be fitted for some new robes and a crozier. Make sure he gets a crozier that's right for his height. I just hate it when one of my bishops looks like he's carrying a tree limb or a walking stick.

CARDINAL: There's a crozier maker in Akron. I'll recommend him. Unless you think he should be encouraged to buy Italian.

POPE: What do you think?

CARDINAL: I'll get right on it.

POPE: Cardinal . . .

CARDINAL: Yes, your Holiness . . .

POPE: Let's not waste this much time on the next one.

The good news is that Father Stottlemaier didn't get the job, so maybe there's room for hope. Anyway, I called him to ask whether or not I could go to a movie. It wasn't just any movie. It was a movie condemned by the Cincinnati branch of the Legion of Decency. The movie got the big C. Not cancer. Condemned. One step up from "morally objectionable in part for all." A condemned movie was the moral nadir. It didn't get any worse than that. And if you saw a condemned movie (an automatic mortal sin) and died before making it to confession (unless, of course, you had made a *perfect* act of contrition), you were off to hell.

Forever. For *eternity*. And how long was that? We knew how long it was, because the Sisters of the Precious Blood told us.

Imagine a bird that comes to earth every ten thousand years. That's ten *thousand* years. And when that bird comes to earth, he picks up one grain of sand from the beach and flies off. That's all, just one. Not a beakful, just one single, solitary grain of sand. You don't see him again for another ten thousand years. (Remember, you're burning in hellfire, in excruciating pain all this while.) By the time the bird has removed all of the sand from all of the beaches on earth, *eternity* has just *begun!*

So there was something at stake here. The list of condemned movies was the most interesting thing in the *Catholic Telegraph Register*, since it listed movies no one had ever heard of before. Where were they showing these movies, and why didn't they ever come to Cincinnati? There were also some weird entries, like this movie in which you actually saw a baby being born. They showed it once at the Twin Drive-In. We saw the previews for it. Somehow it didn't seem very sexy. Just as well, because you wouldn't want to be sent to hell for seeing something that was kind of boring or clinical.

Anyway, the movie I wanted to see was *La Dolce Vita*, the Fellini classic. The very fact that I wanted to see foreign movies was a sign that the rot had started to set in, but I would have thought that the Vatican might cut an Italian director a little slack. But that wasn't the problem. It wasn't the Vatican that stood in my way; it was the archbishop of Cincinnati. His people had put the movie on the list of those carrying the big C.

A couple of years earlier that might have stopped me, but this time I had something going for me (apart from the fact that this was supposed to be a very good movie)—the movie was *not* condemned by the archbishop of Covington. In other words, if you lived on the other side of the beautiful Ohio, you could see the movie. In fact, the archbishop of Covington (somebody promote that man!) had not even claimed that *La Dolce Vita* was morally objectionable in part for all. He had put it in a special category that basically said that this is strong stuff, for a mature audience, but that you could see it without committing a mortal sin. Maybe not even a venial sin.

So here was my problem. One archbishop said a ticket to this movie was a ticket to hell; the other said it offered admission to an experience that might even prove educational. Where was the problem? The problem was that every priest, brother, and sister I had ever had told me that in Catholic teaching morals never change. So what was I supposed to do when morals were changing smack in the middle of every bridge between us and northern Kentucky?

What I did was call Father Stottlemaier. He and I had always gotten along, and, now that he was down at the chancery, I figured he might have a broader view of things. So I called him. And he was there. And he took the call. And he remembered me. And he told me that I couldn't see *La Dolce Vita* because the archbishop of Cincinnati had said the movie was condemned. I was trying to be polite and respectful, but I asked him (in the most polite and respectful way that I could) why the opinion of one archbishop should carry more weight than the opinion of another, and what about the notion of morals changing in the middle of the Broadway bridge?

His answer was long and involved, but it basically consisted of an explanation of the source of the archbishop of Cincinnati's authority, how this came from Rome and how that meant that his authority went back, eventually, to the apostles themselves. (Going to see the movie in Covington wasn't an option, since I was part of the archbishop of Cincinnati's domain, not the archbishop of Covington's.) Since we both knew that the apostles hadn't seen too many movies (and had other problems on their plate, like dealing with Pharisees and Sadducees and dodging Romans and lions), this argument rang a little hollow. We both knew that we were now talking turf and bureaucracy, not faith and morals, and no one wants to believe in a God who will send you to hell for eternity, waiting for that bird to land every ten thousand years, over a jurisdictional distinction.

Anyway, I went to see *La Dolce Vita*, and it was pretty good, especially the scenes dealing with religion—the early shot of the statue of the madonna suspended from the helicopter and, later, the miracle scene. And the scene at the end, with that weird thing on the beach. Powerful stuff. I learned something from it. The archbishop of Covington was on the right track. Maybe they should have made people see it. See just how religious the Italians are, with the Vatican in their backyard. Figure out that the guys in charge weren't always doing so well on their home turf, but that, for some reason or other, they still managed to hold onto their red caps and robes.

So I saw it. But I had the archbishop of Covington protecting me. No small thing. Plus I had my conscience. Always big among the Catholics. Conscience-wise, this one was a no-brainer. And that's where the rot really starts in. When they're threatening hell-fire and that bird who hasn't been seen in one damned long while, you'd think it would be over something clearcut, like—don't kill your neighbor. That's "kill," as in murder. But seeing a movie?

So once you start to question it all, the next step is easier, and the next step is the subject of my story. This time we're not talking *La Dolce Vita.* We're talking *The Night Heaven Fell,* and we're talking Brigitte Bardot. *The Night Heaven Fell* was released in 1957, three years before *La Dolce Vita,* except in Cincinnati, where it hit town later, just in time to put me to the moral test, this time without any support from the archbishop of Covington. So I'm bending the dates a little here. The truth: I had Father Stottlemaier for class in '56 and '57 and called him about *La Dolce Vita* in '60, shortly before *The Night Heaven Fell* hit town, though my doubts about the whole Legion of Decency bag started in '58, so that's when I dated this story.

So the skating on the rim of hell occurred in 1960. Not that *The Night Heaven Fell* was some grind house porno movie. Directed by Roger Vadim, it also starred Stephen Boyd, the guy with the barbed chariot wheels who tried to run Charlton Heston off the track in *Ben Hur.* And it wasn't something really corrupting like *And God Created Woman,* where Brigitte Bardot wore that dress cut low in the back, showing some reverse-cleavage. And I really wanted to see it. The ad in the *Times-Star* promised a lot, and I had always trusted the *Times-Star.*

It was showing at the Guild, the art house that alternated between boring foreign films, which fed the souls of the coffeehouse crowd, and spicy foreign films, which balanced the budget. *The Night Heaven Fell* was somewhere in between, though it tilted toward the spicy. For the archbishop of Cincinnati, however, the decision was easy. The movie was condemned. The big C. Morally objectionable for all. Mortal sin time. Since none of us knew what a *perfect* act of contrition actually consisted of, this meant a race from the Guild to the confessional, with prayers in between that there would be no fatal car accidents.

The one thing we *were* told was that it was highly unlikely that you could make a perfect act of contrition right after committing the sin. After all, the sin had been premeditated, so how could you suddenly experience a moral reversal, say your perfect act of contrition, and be safe? One of my classmates had suggested periodic acts of contrition during the course of the film, but that would surely be seen as bad faith, even if you got up, turned your head away from the screen, and went to the drinking fountain, the refreshment stand, or the men's room.

No, this time if you were in for a dime you were in for a dollar, and that premeditation thing loomed large. It was like the reverse of conscience. Even if you went in with evil intentions and found that the movie was actually boring (or, God forbid, morally uplifting), there were still those evil intentions. Conscience could get you a pass if you could hang tough throughout the process, but if you wavered you were in trouble.

And I was wavering. The movie was condemned, and I was planning to see it. On the conscience side, I had my *La Dolce Vita* experience as a fallback. The archbishop of Cincinnati had been dead wrong (or so my conscience said), and he was probably wrong again. And there were some other things that had accumulated. For example, one night after a Saturday night date, we had gone to midnight mass downtown at St. Louis's and been subjected to a sermon on sexual morality.

It seems the pastor had seen some couples in the parking lot across the street, sitting in their cars, waiting for some time to elapse before mass. Apparently, there was serious kissing going on, and the priest's response was to dredge up memories of Sodom, Gomorrha, Babylon, and other points east. I figured the people couldn't be all that bad if they were going out of their way to go to church, and—who knows—maybe they were even married. That was a long shot, but either way, it didn't seem right that the pastor would run on the way he did, especially knowing that the examples for his sermon were sitting there in church, right in front of him. He was hurting their feelings as well as skating close to a sin of calumny. The lesson I drew (more food for the conscience) was that these guys were too edgy when it came to sex and that God probably had more important things on His mind anyway.

There was that whole business with arousal, after all. It wasn't the deed; it was the consequences. If you could sit in a burlesque house and not be aroused, you were cool. Who could be so lucky? On the other hand, if you couldn't make it through the Sears catalogue without a problem, the Sears catalogue was clearly a near occasion of sin for you, and you had to avoid it. You got a little slack the first time through, since you didn't know that there were corset ads close to the Craftsman wrenches, but the next time through things got serious. The first time, you hadn't consented to the arousal, but the second time, you had already been warned.

There were also guidelines. You were informed, clearly and directly, that no one could experience certain actions (for example, touching a nude female body) without becoming aroused. I often wondered how such things were determined. Was there a testing lab at the Vatican? Who did they perform the tests on? Did they have any vacancies?

And what about women? Women never became aroused. At least hardly ever. Was that fair? What was God thinking when He set up a system like this? It was just too complicated. You couldn't be simpleminded about something as subtle as this (more food for the conscience). You had to add some footnotes, put in some qualifications. We all deserved more slack. Except maybe the women, who had already gotten all the benefits from nature.

And what kind of God would look at reality this way?

St. Louis's Church. The lovers' parking lot is in the left foreground.

GOD: They're in the car.

GABRIEL: Yes, Lord.

GOD: And right across from the church. St. Louis's, right?

GABRIEL: Yes, Lord.

GOD: How long have they been at it?

GABRIEL: Four minutes and thirty-seven seconds, Lord.

GOD: Do we have wood yet?

GABRIEL: We have partial wood, Lord.

GOD: How about the women?

GABRIEL: Cool, Lord. They're still talking about each other's earrings and about what they're going to wear to school tomorrow.

GOD: Any acts of contrition in the pipeline?

GABRIEL: Just the one, coming from the '49 Ford.

GOD: I doubt that we're talking perfection here.

GABRIEL: No, Lord, just a little bet hedging.

GOD: What the hey, I've got to give him points for trying. Most of the time, they wait until they get into the church.

GABRIEL: True, Lord.

GOD: But it's still not *perfect.*

GABRIEL: Certainly not, Lord.

GOD: They always think they can beat the odds, don't they?

GABRIEL: Always, Lord.

GOD: That's why Mo Green went to Vegas.

GABRIEL: I don't know what you mean, Lord.

GOD: Of course, you don't. That's why you've got feathers instead of the big chair.

It couldn't be like that. Besides, Jesus only talked about two commandments, not ten (conscience, are you still there?), and especially not that damned number six and number nine. I needed more help. I couldn't go to the movie by myself anyway, so I called Bob Kramer. He had been my partner in crime in the past. It was Bob Kramer who went with me to the rock and roll shows on school nights. It was Bob Kramer who introduced us to the Protestant girls from Deer Park who used to swear the way the boys did. I asked him if he wanted to go see *The Night Heaven Fell,* and he said, "Sure."

He said it without any hesitation. Maybe my own conscience had become too scrupulous. That was a potential problem that we had been warned about, but, when we asked for examples, Sister Carlotta thought for a long while and then said, strictly by way of example, that some young people might feel that they were committing a sin if they went to church in improper clothes. (Such as without a blouse?) Sister Carlotta said, again by way of example, that some might think it sinful to go in with mismatched socks. Now that would be a sign of a scrupulous conscience. God doesn't care what color our socks are (unless, of course, we're serving mass, in which case we should wear black socks, since they would look right with our cassocks). Again—something the women didn't have to worry about.

Then there was a setback. After Bob Kramer told me "Sure," he'd go, I was starting to relax. Then he said, "What's it about?" I told him it was a Brigitte Bardot movie, and he asked me what it was rated. I hemmed and hawed a little bit and then said, "As a matter of fact, I think this one got the big C." "Really?" he said. "Yes," I answered. Then, to my relief, he said, "OK, what the hell."

So off we went in my car. The statistics said that the passenger seat was the death seat, so in a world of odds I had done myself a little good. The Guild was about a mile and a half from our high school. Our English teacher had taken us there once to see a Shakespeare play that had been turned into a movie. It was our first trip to an art house. When we were there, we saw a marquee still for a sexy French film. He warned us about that possibility before we got there. He said we might see something that could serve as a near occasion of sin, but he also reminded us that it wouldn't pose a problem if we didn't consent to it.

After the movie, he told us that "we had something now that no one could ever take away from us." Culture, I guess. Anyway, it made it easier for us to go to the Guild to see *The Night Heaven Fell.* We were old customers there.

The theater was crowded. Most of the audience were men. We looked around for dirty raincoats but didn't see any. Bob and I went down the right aisle about halfway, took our seats, and stretched out our legs, relaxing. This was no big deal to us. We loved Bardot. Hell, we were old fans from way back, just like the rest of the men there.

The previews were really interesting. There were a lot of movies with subtitles, and there was this one movie that was all about the trial of Oscar Wilde. I thought I might like it, because I really liked trial movies. This one didn't seem to make much sense, though. There was this guy, this really famous writer, and he was on trial. The previews said something about a sin that dared not speak its name. I didn't know what that sin could be, unless it was the sin against the Holy Ghost, which was one of those things we were warned about but had never really had explained to us properly. All of the other sins had been spelled out in great detail. Anyway, the movie showed a lot of people dressed in black clothes, carrying umbrellas, and walking around in the rain, with shocked looks on their faces. I figured I'd take a pass.

There weren't any cartoons or newsreels, serials, or short subjects at the Guild. For that you'd have to go back to Norwood to the Plaza, the Ohio, or the Norwood theaters. This was a theater for adults. Like Bob Kramer and me.

Finally the feature started, and I'm sorry to say that I don't remember much of it. Stephen Boyd played this hit man who was going to kill Brigitte Bardot's uncle or something, and, in the course of the action, he got interested in her. Then they started driving all over Europe in his car. I only remember two things well. The first was a comment from a member of the audience. It came about two-thirds of the way through the movie, after Stephen Boyd and Brigitte Bardot had driven halfway around the world. This guy in the back of the theater suddenly blurts out (and not in any stage whisper; he said it so everybody there could hear), "Jesus Christ, what is this, a Ford road test?"

Everybody laughed. The movie had actually been pretty boring, and that statement was one of the best lines uttered in the theater, even if it came from a member of the audience.

The second thing I remember was the scene that got the movie the C rating. At least we figured that this was the scene that did it, because there weren't any others that could have. The rest of the movie was scenery and driving. In the big scene, Stephen Boyd is standing next to Brigitte Bardot. He's looking into her eyes. She's looking into his eyes. He puts his arms around her. She puts her arms around him. Then he looks into her eyes again. Then she looks into his. Slowly the camera pans down to the ground, and we see her feet for a second. Pretty nice feet, but you wouldn't know that they were Brigitte Bardot's unless you were a real expert. Then, suddenly, her dress falls to the ground, around her ankles, over her feet.

And that was it. That was all of it. That was the whole damned thing. Brigitte took off her dress. Maybe Stephen helped her, but it's clear that she was going along with it. It was what they called a "suggestive" scene. The archbishop must have known that we knew that people who had sex usually took their clothes off first. I mean, she wasn't bored or something and leaving Stephen Boyd to go take a bath. They were getting ready to have sex. We weren't going to see it, of course, but we knew something big was about to happen and the archbishop must have figured that that would plunge us right into the middle of that arousal thing.

Big deal. And it's not as if the movie condoned that dress on the ground and the sex that was probably going to follow. It wasn't as if we were being programmed by Roger Vadim so that every time we'd see a dress (or maybe a red Ford convertible) we'd be suddenly aroused. Hell, we were smarter than that. For example, we knew that Brigitte Bardot was French, so we knew that there'd be some sex happening sooner or later. It wasn't any surprise. It didn't sneak up on us or anything. We took it in stride.

We were more than just boys, after all. We were young *men*. Now we're middle-aged men, and we know much more. For example, we know that a dress around the ankles is something you wouldn't see very often on TV these days, because it would be too tame. And if you did see a dress around the ankles, you'd be very grateful, because your grandchildren could see it without being shocked by any explicit sex. You'd think it was tasteful and decent.

So what does that mean? That morals really do change? Are we back on that bridge again? Or does it mean that we live in Babylon? Does it mean that even though the Legion of Decency is gone, every time we see a dress hit the floor (and nothing else) we're in immediate danger of a one-way trip to hell? Or does it mean that we're allowed to see more and more now because the church can't keep up with it all and has basically punted? Or does it mean that the Legion of Decency was a quaint throwback to the days of the immigrant church and that it's fun to think about in retrospect, even though in its day it (and things like it) may have been responsible for sending a serious number of people to the asylum? Or does it mean that we're now so numb that we've lost all sense of morality?

I honestly don't know. And I don't like to criticize the cardinals for worrying so much about pelvic morality, because I've read the surveys in *Redbook* and *Cosmopolitan* and they say that most of us are thinking about sex all the time, too. All I know is that the fact that *The Night Heaven Fell* was so bland and boring was a godsend. I could walk out of the Guild and make my act of contrition without a moment's hesitation. There was no afterglow of arousal, no warm memory of Brigitte that I couldn't push out of my head; there was nothing, in short, to cloud my thinking. I had broken the rule, and I was really, really sorry. Also, I was out seventy-five cents plus the money for gas. My contrition was as close to perfect as anyone could ask for or imagine.

11

1958–59

Drowning by Numbers

It was the best of beer, it was the worst of beer. I remember the names as if they were members of the family: Wiedemann's, Hudepohl, Schoenling (in longnecks as well as in Little Kings), and Burger. Cincinnati beers. All brewed locally then, before outfits like G. Heilemann and Company started buying up the entire Midwest. There were twenty-eight or -nine functioning breweries in Cincinnati before Prohibition. By the 1950s, only a few remained, though the tradition was a proud one. The beers were sold at restaurants, bars, taverns, road houses, and pony kegs, the last a Cincinnati specialty.

A pony keg (a few survive to this day) is a drive-through structure with cases of beer stacked on skids—golden liquid mountains, lining the walls of elongated garages or steel Quonset huts, looming above the consumer, who drives his sedan or wagon or truck into the center of the enclosure and sits patiently as the vehicle is loaded with serious quantities of his favorite brew.

Beer is both a preprandial and postprandial mainstay of the Cincinnati household. In earlier times, the beer was secured directly from saloons and carried home in jugs, bottles, buckets, or whatever the purchaser had. Hence the term "bucket runners" for steady consumers. Beer was essential for wedding receptions, each hall carrying a particular local brand. It was also an important part of all sporting events, the Crosley Field and Cincinnati Gardens concessions both being important outlets, the bids on them no doubt matters of high politics as well as high finance.

Protective of their brand names and fiercely proud of their local industries, many Cincinnatians rallied to the cause, spurning the allure of products like Budweiser or Schlitz, Blatz, Pabst, Miller, or (much later) Coors or Rolling Rock. Many prided themselves on their available stock of their particular favorite. Thus, basements often featured second refrigerators stocked to the gills with amber bottles. The more dedicated had taps installed in their basements and bought one of the local beers by the keg.

Each was barely drinkable. Wiedemann's was bitter, Schoenling watery, Hudepohl bland and generic, and Burger simply foul. Near-freezing temperatures could ameliorate what was at best a bad situation, as could gimmickry. The Burger people boasted of the smoothness of their beer's bottles, having coated them with a clear sheet of some metallic substance. "Just feel it," the partisans would say. "Run your finger down the sides. See how smooth it is? Look at the bottles. They're not scuffed. Don't you hate that? You know, when the bottles all have those white scuff marks. Burger doesn't have those white scuff marks. Burger bottles are smooth. They're smooth as silk. Here, just slide your finger down the side. Now that is smooth."

"True, but the beer tastes like absolute mule piss."

"Not if it's really cold. And besides, look at how smooth the bottles are."

Once a year there would be bock beer and some temporary distractors like Red Cap Ale or more limited production items like Bavarian's Barbarossa Beer, but the bottom line was that there were basically four beers, and each true Cincinnatian was expected to pass the test of loyalty in the face of judgment and taste. It was a test we easily passed, because our measure of the quality of a bar was not the beer that they had on tap (predictably a local product) but the frequency with which they checked ID cards.

At any given moment, our scouts were scouring the urban landscape, searching for bars or pony kegs that were soft on ID requirements. When they were located and identified, our business was theirs for the taking, and we were prepared to facilitate the continuation of their lawless practices by dressing and behaving as old as our tender years and infrequently shaven faces would permit.

Our pony keg of choice was on Montgomery Road, on the Norwood-Pleasant Ridge border, a small affair next to a hairdresser's, neatly tucked behind the drugstore at the corner of Quatman and Montgomery. To the north was a funeral home, so the snooping pedestrian traffic was both intermittent and otherwise occupied. The pony keg was our carryout source, and the grounds of the local seminary to the south or the stand of trees to the west offered sites for the leisurely consumption of whatever the pony keg had priced for a quick sale.

The bars marked by a more casual approach to legal concerns were clustered in the general vicinity of Silverton and Deer Park, blue-collar neighborhoods to our north, the former the home of the Meier Winery, the Three Boots Tavern, and other genial institutions, the latter the home of a sizable number of my classmates, whose skills as bar scouts were unparalleled.

The bars offered more than beer. Pickled eggs and beef sticks were mainstays, the latter made of appalling ingredients such as beef tripe and beef lips, but delicious both in their spicy individuality and their synergistic relationship with cold draft beer. There were also pork rinds and beef jerky and, on those occasions when the smiles of the gods could be most clearly felt, steam tables piled high with thin slices of roast beef, simmering in juice, ready to be layered on thick slices of homemade rye bread and garnished with sliced dill pickles that could turn the head of the most confirmed and homesick New Yorker.

Ordering was crucial. You listened carefully, watching the regulars, observing their gestures, borrowing their expressions. "A couple of shorts" could work. "We'd each like a glass of draft beer" would land you on the street. You listened for the bartenders' names but didn't push it too hard. "How you doing tonight, Larry?" was four words too many. Instead you nodded. "Larry . . . ," you said, with a touch of tired sympathy after a hard day's work.

A Cincinnati pony keg

Meier's Wine Cellars. The fermentation vats are to the right and rear; the tasting room is still doing a good business.

You knew him. He must know you. If he ever did check IDs, he must have already done it with you, because you knew his name. You were pals. Hell, you went back a long way. And you were careful about the food. You didn't go for the beef sticks or the pork rinds until at least an hour and a half had elapsed. Hunger was a dead giveaway. Kids got hungry. Men drank beer.

One of my favorite drinking partners was Denny Timmins. He was tall and had some recognizable whiskers. He also worked at a nursery after school, so his clothes were stained with dirt and potting soil. Since I had worked construction in the summers, I could talk about doing that work while Denny could look as if he had just done it. We were just a couple of blue-collars stopping in for a drink after a hard day.

"So, yeah, he did it again. We're trying to nail down the damn subfloor, but the chalk line's off because the idiot bumped the string a couple of times instead of just snapping it the way he should of."

"Jesus, I hate when that happens."

"So then we're throwing up the siding, and he starts carrying a sheet of Masonite up the ladder in this high breeze. Like to turn himself into a damn sailboat."

"Ha."

"Two more shorts, Larry."

The reason why a group of sixteen- and seventeen-year-old kids could be seen in bars trying to pass for adults and sometimes succeeding can be summed up in one set of numbers: 3.2 percent. The average beer is 6 percent alcohol (sometimes less, depending on the batch), but the Cincinnati brewers sold 3.2 percent beer, and it was legal for eighteen-year-olds to purchase and consume it. The key was the color of the cap (red vs. blue), and it was a difference that all boys quickly learned.

The principal virtue of 3.2 percent beer (pronounced "three-two") was that you could pretend you were an adult without risk of serious impairment. The common wisdom was that you would drown in 3.2 beer before you would get drunk with it.

This brought with it many civic and social advantages. For example, Coney Island (the Cincinnati version out on the Ohio River) featured a dance pavilion called Moonlight Gardens. Moonlight Gardens was on the edge of the park, just across from the Coney Island version of Lake Como, where canoes could be rented by young lovers.

Moonlight Gardens served 3.2 beer, so young people could go there on weekend evenings, dress up, dance, drink, and slowly begin to turn into adults. It was very popular with the girls (who always seemed to love to dance) and equally popular with the boys (who always seemed to love to drink). Here, both purposes could be served. Moonlight Gardens was open on the sides so that the breezes off the river could mitigate the effects of the Ohio valley humidity, as well as the effects of two or three quarts of beer.

Moonlight Gardens featured large bathrooms on either side of its center stage. These met the needs of the young girls (who travelled to the bathroom in groups to talk and check their makeup) as well as the young boys (who travelled to the bathroom at regular intervals to free their systems of the oceans of 3.2 beer they had consumed).

A further locational advantage of Moonlight Gardens was its position at the edge of the amusement park. There was parking nearby, but it was less desirable than the carefully maintained principal lot at the other end of the park. Thus, when the dancing was finished and the last 3.2 beer had been consumed, the couples could walk through the quiet amusement park to their cars. The distance was such that any lingering effects of the beer were gone by the time you reached your car, and you could drive without any fear of impairment. There was also something romantic in strolling past the ferris wheel, the tilt-a-whirl, the rotor, and the roller coaster structures (the Shooting Star and the Wildcat) in the moonlight.

The rotor, however, carried bad memories for some. A centrifugal-force ride, you entered through a door that was part of the structure of the cylindrical form. Then you took up positions against the wall as the structure began to turn. When it reached sufficient speed, the floor was retracted and you spun around, pinned to the wall in whatever odd position you might choose.

The rotor was perfectly harmless, unless you persisted in lifting your head off the wall, only to have it driven back repeatedly with some force. However, some liked to ride it again and again without regard to possible consequences, and many (myself included) had been on the rotor when someone with a stomach full of cotton candy (or worse) regurgitated it as the structure spun, thus sharing the wealth with all of those unfortunate enough to be along for the ride.

Once past the rotor and the Wildcat, the final vision for those strolling across the park was the light from the vast swimming pool to the parking lot's left, which rippled and danced in the reflected light and helped bring the evening to a close with images of peace and light and calm.

There were other evenings which were less comforting. While most of us survived the effects of the 3.2 beer, indeed even matured with its help, some were less fortunate. Our neighborhood had at least one beeraholic, a boy named Bill Stavers, who spent much of his time in the general area of the Norwood/Pleasant Ridge pony keg. He was not a falling-down drunk, but neither was he completely sober. Eventually, he became a sad fixture for those going to the adjoining drugstore or hair salon.

Beer was not served at our high school dances or at the celebrations which followed our football victories. To say that Purcell High School was strong in football would be an act of considerable understatement. (Factoid: Roger Staubach was our quarterback, but he did not start until his senior year.) The postgame parties in our school gym did not require artificial stimulants or depressants. Our dominance was constant and total (in the days before Moeller High School and its coach, Gerry Faust, came on the scene), and the parties were occasions to walk, talk, smile, and recognize that reality.

One night, we played Central High School, an inner-city school known for its levels of extreme and indiscriminate violence.

We beat them 83–0. On another occasion, we played Boys' Town, beat them decisively, and held them twice on two series of downs that began on the one yard line. We rarely played teams from up-state Ohio, but when we did we took on the powerhouses from places like Canton and Massillon—Paul Brown country.

Our confidence was so complete that our plays were announced to everyone. There were no quarterback running plays. There were minimal passing plays. Basically, we ran around the end, over tack-le, and over guard. The numbers of the plays identified the runner and the hole, and they were sometimes announced loudly enough for the opposing team to hear. Execution, strength, and condition-ing were everything. The plays were so simple and so well known that at sandlot games people would say, "Purcell plays, OK?"

These were not so much games as assertions. They were confir-mations of the Midwestern tenet that anything could be accom-plished with sufficient dedication and effort. To complicate the event with 3.2 beer was entirely unnecessary.

Where we *did* need beer was for the cast parties after our vari-ety shows and plays. The variety shows occurred every spring, and they included girls from local high schools. The performances consisted of singing and dancing, both individually and in groups, and of "variety" acts, e.g., recreating the Danny Kaye "Vessel with the Pestle" bit. The stars of the show were a set of Italian twins from Regina High, who were favored because of their figures as well as their vocalizing. Spilling out of peasant costumes or danc-ing in tights, they always kept my classmates riveted.

We were especially proud of our dramatic presentations because our high school put on real plays, not the goofy written-for-high-school-performers stuff that they did at Regina. We did plays like *Stalag 17* or *The Caine Mutiny Court Martial,* while the nuns at Regina forced the girls to put on crap like *Ramona.* The nuns were also big on subsidiary talents. In *Ramona,* for example, there was a character who played an Indian. In real life, he could play the sax-ophone, so the nuns rewrote the script and put in this cheesy, ridiculous scene in which his "band of Indians" played contempo-rary music.

I got in a bad argument with my current girlfriend over the Regina productions. It was a no-win situation, because if I turned out to be right that would just make her angrier. I told her that the Regina plays were crap and that they should do professional plays the way we did. She denied the charge vociferously, defending *Ramona* as a Broadway-level play. I disagreed and asked her what they were doing next year. She scowled and refused to answer. I pressed her, and she mumbled the words as quickly as she could. I still heard them: the play was going to be *Meet Me at the Prom.*

The parties after the plays *were* professional, which is to say they were what somebody thought of as professional. The girls were all acting as if they had just completed a six-month run at the Winter Garden theater. They were all carrying drinks in their hands, talking in squeaky voices, and kissing everybody who came into the room. This didn't seem to bother any of the boys, who entered into the spirit of the occasion, figuring that anybody who thought actors were sissies didn't know how much beer they drank or how many women they kissed.

It was interesting to watch the girls play a new role like that. Usually they were prim and proper, sometimes chilly, rarely passionate. Somehow being on stage (even in *Ramona*) had turned them into show biz folk. I was in a Holden Caulfield phase at the time and thought the whole business was totally phony, so I stayed on the sidelines, watching it all. I figured the next thing they'd do was start calling each other "darling."

I acted in a couple productions, but I also gravitated toward other duties, developing an interest in makeup. My specialty was constructing beards. The material came in tightly woven, tubular pieces that were three or four inches long. You began by painting clear glue on the underlying facial parts and then pulled out pieces of hairy material, shaped it, and pressed it against the glue. Once you had enough in place, you trimmed it with a scissors and, voilà, an instant musketeer.

The material was easy to work with, and the beards and mustaches looked more and more authentic if the rest of the face was

aged (with accent lines and wrinkles) to match the style of the facial hair. One of our favorite postproduction activities was to install elaborate but plausible beards on each other's faces and then
drive through the carhop restaurants and other public places looking serious, sinister, and generally weird. This wouldn't have
worked in the '60s, but in Norwood in the '50s we looked like
characters from another planet.

We didn't drink beer when we had on our beards. Instead, we'd
try to look as old as possible and then order something that only
kids would eat or drink.

"Yes, sir? What can I get for you?"

"I'd like a glass of milk, a peanut butter and jelly sandwich, and
one of those beanies with the name of the restaurant on it."

"I beg your pardon?"

The trick was to put on lighter wrinkle lines. Stage makeup has
to work under heavy lights, and it has to look right from the tenth,
twentieth, and thirtieth row. Drive-in restaurant makeup has to
look right up close and personal, and the lines are more like subtle
hints than defined shapes or angles. Real pros would also worry
about things like cold-cream smells, but that wasn't much of a
problem for us, since the grill and cooking-grease smells surrounding a drive-in restaurant in Norwood were already compet-
ing with the odors from the Procter and Gamble and Formica
plants blowing in from the west. Under those circumstances, the
heavy scent of cold cream was barely perceptible.

Our impersonations were a nice break from the more serious
occupation of beer drinking. Cincinnatians are a mannerly people
and abide by the rule of seeing that every guest has a drink in his
or her hand before his or her rear end hits a chair or couch. There
is no more severe criticism than the charge that "They just let us
sit there, without offering us something to drink." The elapsed
time between the moment at which one passes through the front
door and the moment in which the drink is finally offered is also
generally noted for the record.

Beer is not the only drink offered, but it is often the drink of
choice, and it is frequently combined with the offer of a ham sand-

wich. Boiled ham is a staple in a Cincinnati refrigerator, as are jars of tangy mustard and loaves of bakery-bought rye bread.

HOST: "What can I get you to drink?"

HUSBAND: "Thanks. I'll take a beer, if you've got some."

HOST: "Absolutely. How about a boiled ham sandwich to go with it?"

HUSBAND: "Oh, I don't know . . ."

WIFE: "Don't tempt him. He doesn't need it."

HUSBAND: "We just ate a little while ago."

HOST: "How about a small one?"

HUSBAND: "Sure."

CHILD: "Daddy, can I have one, too?"

HOST: "Of course, you can. How about you, Marge?"

WIFE: "Oh, why not."

It should be noted that Cincinnati has the best junk food on planet earth, with the sole exception of southern California, and it has the best German-American bakeries, period. The city also has neighborhood butcher shops, where the locals feel free to ask the butcher to clean the grinder before preparing their ground round or ground chuck. The ham is always something special; the Kahn's hot dogs are justifiably advertised as "the wiener the world awaited"; and the bratwurst are better than those from Milwaukee. Only the beer is bad, but as long as it's served cold . . .

Even today my mother keeps a set of antique beer mugs in her kitchen cabinet for my visits. The glass is paper thin, but it can be frosted without serious risk to the integrity of the mug. When she offers me a beer, the ice is literally falling off the mug in tiny sheets.

My father-in-law is a bourbon drinker, but his refrigerator is always full of beer for his guests, though he himself only drinks it occasionally. The brand is always Wiedemann's, and he never has less than thirty cans on hand.

One night many years ago, he told me that he felt like drinking some beer, and he asked me if I was thirsty. I said, "Sure," and volunteered to go down to the refrigerator in his cellar to get us some Wiedemann's. "No," he said, "I know a place on the river that has good beer on tap."

The saloon was a place called Schulte's, and it was downriver, toward Addyston. On a rise just above River Road, it was strictly a local hangout. There was no dartboard, no pool table, no slot machine, no pinball machine, no punchboard, and no TV. The building sign was dim, and the parking lot was small, so you had to know the neighborhood in order to find it. There was no truck traffic and no outsiders who were just passing through. The main room held about five or six tables with eight seats at the bar. On the right side, there were two small tables in a smaller room that was more of a breezeway to the telephone, the coatrack, and the toilets than anything else.

The place was old and dark, but it was clean. My father-in-law informed me that every good saloon would have its taps cleaned daily, but that this place often had it done twice a day. "He sells a lot of beer," my father-in-law said. The owner's name wasn't Schulte. The Schultes were long gone, though their name remained. The current owner's name was Lou Becker.

I had never heard my father-in-law mention the place before. Indeed, I had never seen him drink more than a single glass of beer at any one time. Tonight, however, he said he had a taste for it. When we entered, the bartender called my father-in-law by name, and my father-in-law introduced me both to the bartender and to two or three of the other patrons. They were post office people, and they all knew my father-in-law, who had been director of delivery for the city of Cincinnati, a regional officer for the tri-state area, a vice president of the retired federal employees' association, and postmaster of both Louisville and Cleveland. In the 1960s, he was offered the position of directory of delivery for the entire United States. He could never do anything untoward or embarrassing because he could never appear on a street or in an alley of greater Cincinnati for more than ten or fifteen seconds without having at least two people recognize him and call him by name.

The bartender asked us what we wanted, and we both said "Draft." I was always told that it was impolite to watch people eat or drink and to keep count of what they had consumed, but that night I couldn't help myself. We sat in that saloon for at least five hours, during which time my father-in-law drank at least two gallons of beer. I tried to keep up, but the only way I could stay on the barstool was to have two hamburgers, some French fries, chips, peanuts, pork rinds, Slim Jims, and just about everything else the bartender sold.

After the first hour, I started wearing a path between the bar and the men's room and eventually settled into a twenty-minute cycle. My father-in-law didn't have anything to eat, and he never left the barstool. Every fourth drink or so was on the house, and every fifteen or twenty minutes the bartender would ask if we wanted the next one warmed up. By that he meant did we want a shot of whisky in between beers. My father-in-law had a couple of them, but eventually he said that he really wasn't thirsty for whisky, he was just thirsty for beer.

Just before they had to call for a gurney to get me back to the car, he asked me if I wanted anything else. I said no, thanks. He sat for just a second, thinking about it, and then said, "Oh hell, let's go on home. I've got plenty of beer there if we decide that we want some more."

We walked to the car. I was doing my best impersonation of sobriety while he was steady as a rock. After we got into the car and he started to pull out of the lot, he said, "You know, when I was a young man I really liked to drink beer, but now I just have a few glasses every now and then, like tonight."

I have never seen him drunk. I have never even seen him tipsy. When he was young, he liked to fish in northern Michigan. One day, I asked him if he had ever done any ice fishing, and he said yes, but that he didn't care for the cold, since you had to carry so much whisky with you to sustain yourself while you were out there. He told me that he and his friends used to take a case of whisky with them every time they went out on the ice. I asked him if he took some food along, too, and he said, "Oh, of course. We usually took a box of Hershey bars." He is a real Cincinnatian, and the rest of us are just aspirants.

12

1959

Twinkletoes

All happy and unhappy adolescents are alike in the same ways. They all need a clearer complexion, a better sense of balance, a surer sense of themselves, a modicum of respect from members of the opposite scx, and some special help in preparing for adulthood. The latter is particularly important because adolescents are often difficult as a class. Knowing that fact, the most they can often hope for is something between minimal tolerance and benign neglect.

What they need is something or someone to trust, since very little appears to work in their day-to-day experience of themselves, and the world which limns and colors and sometimes seems to envelop their lives. This is particularly true in high school, that special portion of hell where the comforts of grammar school have all been lost and the freedoms of college have not yet been discovered.

With a single exception, each of my grammar school classmates went to Purcell High School. Named for Archbishop Purcell, a shadowy figure about whom nothing of note was ever said, the school was run by the aforementioned Marianists, a Catholic religious order which arose at the time of the French Revolution and later operated schools from Long Island to Honolulu. It was all male, just as the corresponding women's school, Regina, was exclusively female.

The chichi high school in Cincinnati was Xavier, "St. X" or

sometimes just "X," the Jesuit school. It suffered from several major deficits: it was downtown; it was expensive; and, most unacceptable to us, its students did not change rooms for classes. One of the signal changes in our academic lives, a marker on the path to intellectual maturity, was the freedom to get up and walk around between classes, an opportunity denied by the Xavier system.

"Where you goin'?"

"Purcell, I guess."

"Why?"

"X is too expensive. Besides, you don't get to change rooms between classes."

"No shit?"

"No shit."

"What a pain. What's the point in leaving grade school?"

"None. Besides, it's downtown."

"What a pain. Riding the bus all the way down there."

"Right. Plus my parents say it's too expensive. And then you don't get to change rooms between classes."

Purcell was a football powerhouse; I've already mentioned the fact that Roger Staubach was our *second*-string quarterback until his senior year. It was so-so in every other sport, except perhaps intermural bowling, but compared with football nothing else really mattered anyway. Cincinnati may have been a basketball town, with Xavier University (Cornelius Freeman), the University of Cincinnati (Jack Twyman, Oscar Robertson), and the nearby University of Dayton (Johnny Horan), all fielding their best teams ever, but football was the manly sport for those whose manhood was not yet a certainty. Purcell was nothing if not manly. It is fair to say that, though it was not a school for toughs, it was still a tough school. It continues to give me some sense of reassurance that most of the unpleasant people with whom I occasionally have to deal would not have lasted more than a week there.

Freshmen were routinely hazed. The hazing lasted for a prescribed length of time: namely, until the upperclassmen grew tired of it. At pep rallies, each class was formally introduced and then announced its presence through the emission of a thunderous scream. ("Gentlemen, I give you the members of the class of 1959—the lords of the Cavalier Castle, the SENIORS!") The members of the freshman class were referred to as "the denizens of the peanut gallery" (an allusion to the little kids' bleachers on the Howdy Doody Show) or "the charter members of the Mickey Mouse Club" (an allusion to the Disney TV show that featured songs, dances, cartoons, and twelve-year-old girls' incipient breasts). The freshmen were sold elevator passes and swimming-pool memberships, though the building contained neither. One of the favorite routines of the upperclassmen was to lock arms across the stairwells after the lunch break and move very, very slowly, thus panicking the freshmen who feared demerits, detention, and the other fates awaiting those who were late for class.

Each locker was secured by a regulation padlock, and upper-classmen had an uncanny ability to discover other peoples' combinations. This led to several results: the trashing of the lockers' contents, the "frenching" of locks (that is, reversing the lock's position and wedging it against the metal door so that the numbers could not be read by the person trying to open it), and—the most feared action of all—the switching of a whole group of locks along a corridor, so that the freshmen were forced to both cooperate with one another and give away their combinations in an effort to open their lockers quickly, secure their books or other materials, and get to class on time.

Another favorite pastime of the upperclassmen was to goose unsuspecting freshmen in the stairwells and laugh at their overre-actions. This could be dangerous, since the accidental goosing of an upperclassman could lead to serious reprisals, while the overre-action of a tripping or falling freshman could lead to the general collapse of all of those near him. The steps were steep and made of heavy tile, so the collapse of a dozen or more individuals could re-sult in significant injuries. The general action of goosing was par-ticularly offensive to the administration, which campaigned against the behavior, referring to instances of the activity as "im-pure practices," a description which managed to confuse most of

Purcell High School, now Purcell Marian. The Twinkletoes tree was just to the left of the principal structure.

the students, who found it both too hopeful and too ambiguous. One was not likely to waste whatever allotment of impure practices was permitted on freshman boys.

Shirts and ties were mandatory, though uniforms were not. Smoking was strictly forbidden, the basis for immediate suspension. There was a liberal arts curriculum and a business curriculum. The first was designed for students planning to attend college; the second was designed for students planning to go to work. The business curriculum contained more interesting students. Most were tough; nearly all were worldly-wise.

My most memorable teachers were Brothers Klune and Zelder. Brother Klune taught Typing I and II, and he did it creatively. There were exercises and timed tests of various kinds. The granddaddy of them all was to be chosen to type on the electrified typewriter on Brother Klune's desk. It was not an electric typewriter. It was a modified Underwood, wired to a large, framed keyboard model above the blackboard. Every time you hit a key on Brother Klune's machine, the corresponding letter or symbol would light up on the model. The point of the exercise was to type quickly, accurately, and rhythmically. If you didn't, that fact was immediately apparent to all of your classmates. One other thing—Brother Klune claimed that if your fingertips slipped between the keys you would get an electric shock.

To my knowledge that was not true, but fear sharpened everyone's attention. Stupidities and misbehaviors were immediately greeted with the title of "Knucklehead," "Bonehead," or, when Brother Klune was in a German literary mood, "Hans Wurst!" Playing with the machines was strictly forbidden, and infractions were strictly enforced. The usual response was the removal of the typewriter from your station and the highly dramatized substitution of a rattle or sugar pacifier in its place.

Typing class also included basic instruction in the preparation of business correspondence and the conveying of such knowledge as the technique for achieving perfect paper folds. When the basic skills were mastered, we moved on to their refinement. Brother Klune believed in typing to music with prominent metronome sounds in the background. He also believed in accuracy approaching perfection. The result was a high level of competence and self-confidence. If you could survive Brother Klune, you could type with the professionals, which is to say the women. Brother Klune regaled us with constant stories of the physical strength of professional typists, shaming us by the implicit comparison with otherwise frail women and urging us to perceive strong, steady typing as a macho activity.

His favorite story concerned a woman who typed eight hours a day, forty hours a week on a standard Royal typewriter. Her husband was a pipefitter; one day when she was on the construction site with him, the vise which was used to hold the pipe in place for the cutter broke. The woman (she was small in stature, Brother Klune stressed) told her husband that that would not be a problem. She walked up, took the pipe in her hands, secured it in a death grip, and told the cutter to cut away. We sat there, our mouths agape, wondering if our own fingers and wrists would ever become such lethal instruments.

I was personally so pleased with what I had learned in Brother Klune's class that I told him that I was considering taking his business machines class the next year. He dissuaded me, commenting that I should take a liberal arts elective instead. He also told me that the business machines class was designed for students who were prepared to work hard, and he knew that I would have difficulty doing that. I told myself that that was his way of helping me to focus on my goal of attending college. I had done reasonably well in the class, receiving two medals donated by the Underwood corporation, but no one envied me that position, because Brother Klune's liberally distributed criticism and consistently applied punishments served their purpose of keeping all young egos in harness.

Brother Zelder taught Latin IV and Calculus. We considered him to be highly intelligent, not just because he taught those particular subjects but also because he was from New York, the praises of whose regents' exams he regularly sang. He was always nice to me, letting me back into Sodality after I was dismissed from it in junior year because of a "bad attitude." He listened to my then chronic complaints, put them in perspective, and directed me toward higher thoughts and activities.

He never lied to us, and he never obfuscated. I asked him once about a former teacher's leaving the Marianists, a fact that had been hushed up with great skill and assiduity. He was as open with me as anyone could have been in those days. I asked him about release from permanent vows and how that could be possible if the vows were truly permanent. He told me candidly that he did not think anyone could really be released from such vows, not if they were taken in the presence of the Blessed Sacrament. In later years, I found this very reassuring, particularly when sympathetic Boston cardinals were running interference for the wealthy in search of annulments and other church actions.

I learned later that Brother Zelder had himself left the Marianists. That did not shock me nearly as much as the fact that he ended up working in the advertising business in Atlanta, not that there is anything illegal or immoral in that, but it seemed too great a distance from the teaching of Latin IV and Calculus.

Several of my classmates joined the Marianists, but most eventually left. I considered it for a time but decided against it when I realized that the members of the order were all human. I knew I could get that on the outside.

Part of my fascination with the religious life had to do with pool tables. We loved pool, but, with the exception of the array of tables at the American Legion Bowling Alley in Pleasant Ridge, pool tables were always found in disreputable neighborhoods with disreputable owners and disreputable clienteles. The sole consistent exceptions were the domiciles of the Marianists. Whether in Cincinnati, Dayton, or wherever, the Marianists' houses always had a pool table. Thus, if you joined the Marianists, you could spend the rest of your life playing pool.

This was not an insignificant fact. The Marianists also had basketball hoops, not the bent kind without a net, but regulation, netted hoops. Wherever we sought to play, there were always too many kids for the available baskets. The result was something more like rugby than basketball. The sole exceptions were those occasions when we visited the Marianists. There we could play in a civilized fashion, and we could play any time we wanted to play. If you joined the Marianists, you could, in fact, spend the rest of your life playing basketball.

The Marianists' houses always included a large sitting room filled with couches and overstuffed chairs. After dinner, the priests and brothers repaired to the sitting room to read the evening paper and take their leisure. Totalling up the collective fringe benefits afforded by membership in the order, it became clear that this was the closest that any of us would come to joining a real gentlemen's club, a club with couches, newspapers, pool tables, and basketball hoops.

There was also the little matter of those vows of poverty, chastity, and obedience, but they were not fully understood at the time, and the pool tables were powerful counterweights. What does it mean to take a vow of poverty when you live in a big house with all of the features of the Clue mansion? What is obedience? We had never really much practiced it ourselves, and we had never seen any instances of Marianists being ordered around by their superiors. It wasn't as if they were in the army or the Teamsters. Chastity was a problem, but all that pool and basketball burned energy and created a nice distraction.

I mulled these things over for a year and a half. Then Twinkletoes arrived, and my decision was made. But first a word or two about Archbishop Purcell High School BT, that is, before Twinkletoes. The principal was a priest named Kerr, whose brother, Walter Kerr, was the drama critic for the *New York Times*. Our Father Kerr was not a theatrical man, but he was warm and outgoing. He was also steadfastly honest and scrupulously fair.

His assistant for discipline was a Marianist brother named Lawrence Eveslage, who was (and still is) called Brother Larry. Brother Larry was tall, tough, witty, tough, sympathetic, and tough. Whenever you were given demerits by a member of the faculty, you had to present yourself to Brother Larry, hand him the demerit ticket, and endure "the look." The look was sometimes accompanied by words, but the words were always superfluous. The look began by boring into the center of your forehead, moving on to the cortex, then progressing to the heart and stomach before it returned to the mouth and lips, resulting in fluttering, sweaty, incoherent promises to do better in future days.

Brother Larry supervised the detention room, which he regularly entered in a state of preoccupied frustration. Two things were always clear: Brother Larry would mete out every last measure of punishment that you deserved, and he would do so in a spirit of concern and affection that was free of darker motives. I am delighted to report that he is still alive and is the most effective basis for fundraising in the history of Purcell High School. No one who ever met Lawrence Eveslage came away without feeling the most profound respect and affection for him, particularly in those moments in which he was administering the punishments which we so richly deserved.

Father Kerr was also respected and even loved, but he was constrained by the chores of the file cabinet, the in-box, the always ringing telephone, and the public lectern. He had neither the time nor the opportunity to involve himself in his students' personal lives. That duty fell to Brother Larry. Father Kerr never hid behind him, never scapegoated him, and never undercut him. They complemented one another, respected one another, and worked together with a striking degree of effectiveness, anticipating one another's reactions, generally agreeing on a course of action after an exchange of no more than a sentence or two.

Father Kerr tended toward the jolly, Brother Larry toward the wry. Father Kerr was the master of the rolling period, Brother Larry the technician of the single, piercing adjective. Father Kerr's good humor was always in his eyes and on his lips. Brother Larry's was beneath the surface, but no less apparent.

They drew boundaries that could not be crossed, but they took a silent delight in watching us dance along those boundaries' edges. They perceived the relationship between learning and discipline and kept the two in subtle balance, maintaining more than adequate order within a small building containing twelve hundred boys.

It was not perfect. It was not idyllic. Though the Cavalier Castle, as it was awkwardly termed, was ultimately safe, it could be rough at the edges. There were suspensions and occasional expulsions and, now and again, the rare fistfight, but order was preserved, an order that was neither fascistic nor dull. In retrospect, it worked brilliantly, and it worked brilliantly because at the heart of the enterprise—no matter what the noise or level of devilment at the borders—there was a center of unwavering trust, trust in the enterprise, trust in the traditions of the school, but most of all, trust in two men.

Their responses were predictable, their values clear. One day in civics class, a kid from the west side of town used the word "nigger" in an open discussion. He was more than tough; he was an out-and-out criminal who usually watched his behavior in class because the pressures of his evening job and its time commitments could not be sacrificed to an hour or more of detention. That job consisted of the systematic theft and fencing of automobile drive shafts.

The civics teacher that day was actually a student teacher from a local college. He was gaunt and somewhat awkward. When the kid, whose name was Charlie Kress, uttered the word, the civics teacher freaked. He paused for a moment, composed himself, and ordered Charlie Kress out of his room. Permanently. On the spot. That very instant. The moment the teacher made that decision, we knew that it was final. Charlie would not be back in that civics class. And if he attempted to confront the student teacher (it was clear he had been testing his limits with him and had crossed the line), he would be dealing, instantly, with Brother Larry, who would treat him fairly and decently but give no quarter. And if he tried to press Brother Larry, as he had tried to press the student teacher, his clock would be cleaned so quickly that whatever was left of him would have to be scraped up with a spatula.

Into that world came a man named Matthew Forrest. Father Matthew Forrest. "Call me Father Matthew." He was tall and wispy and tripped slowly down the hallways like a suspicious dancer. We called him Twinkletoes.

Matthew Forrest was our new principal. His every step was unpredictable, his values indiscernible. His responses to pointed questions were always weasel-worded. He worked by indirection, pitting one individual against the other, recruiting ferrets and informants, watching eyes, testing reactions.

He fancied himself a speaker, though most of his rhetoric had a tinny echo to it and most of his words were either hyperbolic or overly guarded. He had made a minor reputation as a retreat master, and he hoped to use those experiences to advantage in his new role. It was not a good tactical move. We had little use for retreats and retreat masters.

Some of us had stopped by Gethsemani on a history club trip (one of our major disappointments being that we did not see Thomas Merton while we were there), and, though we did not spend more than a few hours within the monastery, we had seen enough to know that this was the real thing. The other retreat houses were largely a mixture of cheesy pamphlets, maudlin sermons, and unnatural silences. When our class became seniors and went on retreat, it was to the third retreat house in as many years, since the previous classes had each smuggled in beer, cards, and other sources of relief sufficient to have our school banned in perpetuity.

This, of course, became a badge of honor and each succeeding class felt called upon to set a new standard of recalcitrance in the face of tepid piety. We had little use for the likes of Twinkletoes and his world. That in itself might have saved him, for whatever sense of fairness we possessed had been inculcated by Brother Larry, and his lessons usually stuck. We knew that we didn't like game players like Twinkletoes. The one thing upon which all could agree was that we had zero tolerance for anyone who might attempt to manipulate us or jerk us around. However, we knew that we could be a difficult lot, and we knew how our behavior had been received by Father Kerr and Brother Larry. We might just have learned from that experience and cut him the tiniest bit of slack.

It didn't happen. It didn't happen because Twinkletoes crossed the line. If he had persisted in his childish deviousness, we might have counterattacked in kind but stopped short of threatening scorched-earth reprisals. He chose, however, to raise the stakes. He did what no one, least of all an outsider, was permitted to do: Twinkletoes frightened our women.

What he did was serve as master for an in-house retreat at Regina High School. Master was the kind of word he liked seeing after his name, and he played the role with avidity. The theme of his retreat was purity, and the subject was sex, pure and simple. Basically, there were two strategic approaches to discussions of sexual morality. The first was more general. That approach talked about things like adultery (not a major option for us, as a rule), pornography, self-abuse (the very phrase redolent of philosophic possibility), kissing, petting (a nice word, after all, though both imprecise and overused as a euphemism), and intercourse (the last lacking any modifying adjectives, since it was still 1958–59 and Cincinnati). This list could be refined slightly, with discussions of such activities as so-called "soul kissing," a nice Catholic euphemism, though unclear in its meaning to nonpractitioners.

The second approach was far more clinical and got into questions, for example, of complete and incomplete pleasure, pace Mick Jagger, for whom the former remains an unattainable ideal. We were certainly of his party, since any pleasure we took was usually accompanied by so much guilt and confusion that any notion of completeness remained remote. This approach combined casuistry with questions of physiologic response. The prior approach, for example, would have considered any "petting" dangerous, but "heavy petting" always mortally sinful. The second approach, on the other hand, measured petting on the complete/incomplete scale. It was more concerned with the response to stimuli. If light, brotherly fondling did not induce serious arousal (again, measured against some absolute scale), the resultant sin might well be venial. Here the less easily aroused had a clear advantage, a moral approach which ran the decided risk of privileging the experienced over the inexperienced.

The degree of casuistry could increase with the addition of clinical detail. For example, if one were unexpectedly aroused, i.e., aroused beyond the degree expected to accompany the behavior in question, and studiously avoided consent to that arousal, the degree of moral turpitude might be adjusted accordingly. Considering the fact that this youthful control group could be expected to be among the most premature of all ejaculators, this particular line of moral inquiry led to a seemingly endless discussion of the decidedly problematic case of the nonconsenting individual passing (with absolute reluctance) the physiological state that bore the highly technical and highly clinical title of the "point of no return."

Given our parents' experience in the war, particularly for the sons of aviators in the South Pacific, this phrase added military metaphor to a situation that was already nearly as frightening and as stimulating as combat. However, since combat was a remote experience for this control group, it was a fair casuistical point to look to inexperience (certainly on the first occasion of the occurrence) as a mitigating circumstance.

Twinkletoes followed neither of these approaches in his sermons with the women of Regina. Instead he opted for drama—high drama, doubtless, in his own opinion. His goal was to present the situation of a misguided couple through their own preferred lenses, then to expose the realities of the situation to the cold light of moral reality.

He did this with the aid of gesture, intonation, and grimace, and all were overdone:

HE: "I love you."

SHE: "No you don't. You just love the ... *t i n g l e s*."

HE: "No, I really love you."

SHE: "Really?"

HE: "I want to be with you forever."

SHE: "Do you really?"

HE: "Yes, of course I do."

FATHER: "He didn't love her. He doesn't love her. He loves the tingles! What is he really saying when his lips mouth the words 'I love you'? He's saying, 'God damn you to hell!' What is he saying when he tells her he wants to be with her forever? He's saying, 'I want you in hell forever!' If you ask them what happened, he'll say he blames her, and she'll say she blames him. What really happened? They both sinned. God blames them both!"

The result of the performance was a feeling of fear bordering on terror and the association of the physical expression of what might sometimes actually be love with that fear and terror. The

Regina women were neither impressed with Father Matthew Forrest's morality nor his oratory, and they wrote a group letter announcing that fact. In the words of the sexual harassment code,
Father Matthew Forrest had proven himself to be the creator of
a hostile atmosphere. Moreover, he had shown some signs of
relishing the role. The flashing eyes and the abrupt hand move-
ments, the Old Testament tones in which he uttered the word
"damn," and the curious facility he possessed of stretching the
word "t i n g l e s" to what felt like at least four syllables—all these
behaviors indicated a level of psychic involvement far beyond the
requirements of the situation.

For us, the sulfurous speech at the Regina retreat was one action in a growing list of actions. Who was this man? How could
he come to represent the church? Worst still, how could he come
to represent the Marianists? For me personally, Matthew Forrest
was the final indication that I required to confirm my realization
that the members of this particular religious order could not only
be depressingly human but, in this case at least, decidedly beneath
the common norm.

I began to wonder how I could ever consider joining an organization that offered what I could already find on the outside without giving up my car, my earnings, and my girlfriend. If I were to
give them up, I had reasoned, I might find something purer,
sweeter, and more spiritual. What I found in Twinkletoes Forrest
was all of the pettiness, the meanspiritedness, and the not very
carefully cloaked violence of the outside world, wrapped in a robe
of self-righteous, holier-than-thou (and, probably, libido-repress-
ing) abusiveness.

And then something happened. It was one of those restorative
moments, the kind that sometimes come when we are at low ebb
and count for much more as a result. I was walking into school one
morning when I heard sounds coming from the adjoining schoolyard. That portion of the Purcell grounds was a very special place.
On each day when weather permitted, we took a walk in the
schoolyard after lunch. The cafeteria featured the usual barely
chilled milk, overcooked vegetables, heavy starches, and mystery

meat items, but, being Cincinnati, it also offered an additional choice—huge baskets full of soft pretzels, which were sold two for a nickel.

These were the real thing—soft and fresh and salty, glistening with brine—the same kind of soft pretzels that were sold on street corners downtown in small brown paper bags, not some institutional-food knockoff. After lunch, we would pick up a pair of pretzels and head for the schoolyard, eating and talking and taking our leisure. It was our commons room, our gentlemen's club, and the schoolyard brought us together, offering fresh air, defusing tension, and providing, on its asphalt, some fraction of what our English counterparts must have felt in their school gardens.

At the east end of the yard, there actually was a garden, or at least a grassy area with a huge tree, a shrine to Mary, and some shrubs. And up in the tree, on that fine morning, there was a rope, a rope hanging from a high limb. And at the end of that rope, ten feet or more above the ground, there was an effigy of Matthew Forrest. It wasn't a simple set of sticks and rags. It was a full figure, and across its form, in large block letters, was the word "Twinkletoes."

I had heard of effigies and read of them in books, but here was the genuine article. There was a buzz running through the crowd, but it was subdued—a single, earnest hum. The faculty discovered the effigy after the students did, and they were aghast. Someone made a call, and the school janitor appeared, carrying a huge ladder. He positioned it against the tree and began to climb.

The effigy was high, and the knots securing it were sure ones. The janitor struggled with them as the effigy swung back and forth. The crowd was suddenly silent. There were no cheers or catcalls. Our minds were pondering the enormity of the act and its possible consequences. Someone had actually stood up, determined that this could go no further, and proceeded to hang the principal in effigy. In doing so, he had risked certain dismissal. Instant dismissal. Unappealable dismissal. Someone had felt that strongly and acted that decisively. What would be the final result of it all?

The janitor tugged and jerked and shook, pulling so hard that we worried that he might endanger himself atop the ladder. When he pulled again, this time abruptly, the effigy came loose. The janitor's motion, however, had been too strong. The effigy was not so much released as it was jerked out of position, and, when it fell, it did not fall directly to the ground but rather in a gentle arc; it fell into a garbage can positioned to the side of the tree, a garbage can for the schoolyard's collected refuse.

It fell like the purest jump shot in double overtime. It fell without a trace of net. And when it fell, disappearing into the trash can, the crowd suddenly erupted in a cry of joy. We all stood there watching but struggling to believe our eyes.

The aftermath was sweeter still. Matthew Forrest was transferred immediately, disappearing into history like a diver in a distant lake. Moreover, no effort was made to find the effigy's creator. No accusations were filed. No questions were asked. This man had come in and nearly destroyed our school, and one of our classmates had decided that that was something that could not be permitted. Somewhere within the hierarchy, whether that of the order, the diocese, or the church (we never knew, of course), someone had realized the mistake that had been made and rectified it. That person or person further recognized that the creator of the effigy was, in some measure, a public benefactor, perhaps not to be celebrated but certainly not to be persecuted. That gave all of us hope and, since giving us hope, more or less, was a significant part of the order's, the diocese's, and the church's job, we all felt, if only for a few moments, that none of us need ever suffer at the hands of a needy ego in search of prey. The event suggested that those who would control our world were sometimes capable of responding to a just voice and that, for a single spring morning and perhaps for the days beyond, things could actually be set right.

13

1957/1997

Charles Hardin Holley and
the Infant of Prague

At Purcell, we did not associate the word "sophomore" with its etymological connotations of "wise fool"; to us, it meant we were something other than (thank God) freshmen. Hell year, with its assorted indignities, was now behind us. We were free to join the ranks of the upperclassmen and enjoy the rights and privileges accruing thereto.

The next year we were juniors, wondering what another year would bring. It proved to be an interesting one. It started in a bizarre way and become progressively more curious as the sheets of the calendar broke loose and fell away. September's strangest fad was the development of a private language by Timmy Carson, a kid from the east side of Deer Park. Timmy was a classic survivor in a tough neighborhood—short in stature, usually dressed in black slacks and shirt, chronically borrowing cigarettes, he depended on his wits to get him through the gauntlets he regularly faced.

The language he created went through Purcell like a virus in a weakened village. The summer had been too hot and too short, and the whole school was looking for a diversion to help get through the academic inevitabilities of the early fall. Timmy's language was the perfect antidote to mental discipline and Catholic regimentation. Basically, it depended on a series of repeating prefixes and suffixes, with heavy doses of assonance. A long u sound, for example, connoted "fat," a short *e* sound "thin." These were coupled with prefixes commonly beginning with the letter *l.* Thus, a fat kid named Bob became "the lit-u Bob-u," while a thin kid named Brent became "the lenty Brenty." The short *i* sound could substitute for the short *e,* as needed, with *t*'s added for internal alliteration. Thus, Tim himself was "the linty Timty," underplaying his own weight while he magnified the weight of others.

There were also some bathroom-humor nouns. Timmy defined a "frump" as any person who "lets farts in the bathtub and then bites the bubbles," a term he regularly applied to those who called him "the lit-u Tim-u." A "guppy" (this one counterintuitive) was a form of superfrump, while a "quigley" was defined as a guppy's uncle, a slightly smaller quigley being designated through the use of a diminutive suffix: thus, a "quigleyma."

Needless to say, one had to have been there. But we all had been, and the effects of the unnamed language were sweeping, with half the school mimicking Timmy and trying to get each phrase and inflection dead solid perfect. Timmy, of course, moved on to new phrases, new grammatical forms, and new vowel sounds as quickly as the former ones became commonplace. It was his role in life to dwell acutely at the cutting edge of all time-wasting activities, and no one challenged his pride of place. To the Deer Park toughs, he was by turns a mascot or jester; to the Purcell underclassmen, a strange god from a foreign clime.

Timmy Carson's private language was succeeded in the fall by Johnny Cox's newest form of selective violence. Cox was a greaser bully whose goal in life was to bring subordinate boys as close to tears as their young manhood would permit. This year he accomplished his goal in gym class by grabbing the bare calves of weaker boys with his fingernails and then proceeding to squeeze and pull until he either left welts or drew blood. He called these assaults "horsebites," and they quickly spawned a series of copycat actions by other bullies. For weeks, people walked cautiously across the hardwood floor with their chins on their shoulders, trying to protect themselves from attack.

The horsebites finally stopped when a fat kid named Joey Bratton grabbed Cox and tried to hit him. The swing was wide, but Joey lost his balance and fell on Cox, knocking the wind out of him, scaring the bejesus out of him, and pummeling his Vitalis-slicked head against the polished oak gym floor. The best thing was that, even though Joey's leg was bleeding, he hadn't shed a tear. When he got to his feet, a couple of the kids even patted him on the back as Cox skulked away. One called out, "the lit-u Joe-u!" The context of the victory had suddenly turned Timmy's form of taunt into a high compliment.

By winter, we were taking trips with the History Club, which Bob Kramer and I were finally eligible to join. The History Club was the brainchild of Father Harvey Wintermeuler, a balding diocesan priest with a taste for the better things. One of those things was his '57 Oldsmobile, a factory hot rod which was the Oldsmobile equivalent of the 270 Chevy. It came with three two-barrel carburetors (the linkage for which constantly required adjustment) and other refinements.

Wintermeuler's tastes were financed by sales tax stamps. In those days in Ohio, you received printed, colored stamps featuring the state seal (larger than postage stamps but smaller than bus transfers) every time you purchased an item and paid the mandatory sales tax. These were redeemable by charitable organizations (not individuals) at a rate that was a minuscule fraction of their face value. For example, if you paid a dollar for something and paid three cents in sales tax you got a three-cent sales tax stamp. When you accumulated $100 worth of sales tax stamps (requiring gross purchases of over $3,000), you could redeem them for $3. To get a hundred bucks in cash, in other words, you had to spend about a hundred thousand dollars.

Every time you purchased a car or anything sufficiently large to land you on a mailing list, you were solicited by charitable organizations for your sales tax stamps. Ours, however, always went to Father Wintermeuler, whose supply sources and collection strategies were among the most advanced we had yet encountered. They generally involved a none too subtle balance of coercion and cooptation. He was grading our American History papers, after all.

However, some of the proceeds were kicked back to his students in the form of subsidized trips for the members of the History Club, which we, of course, promptly joined. Suddenly, we were working for ourselves and not just for the man.

It was on such a trip that we visited Gethsemani Monastery and tried, unsuccessfully, to meet Thomas Merton. (He was there, we were told, but unavailable.) Neat place. Good cheese. We got a tour from one of the superiors, a vice abbot or something, who filled us in on what the monks "had been told" lately, that is, what they were permitted to know about the outside world. This struck us as an eminently sensible system. Most of what was going on in the outside world was pretty crappy anyway, and we thought it was cool to have somebody screen the stuff for you, so you could keep your head clear and quietly drive your tractor or make cheese.

(That was my first and only abbot, by the way. Years later, when I was working at a Catholic university, the president's office issued a set of rigid directions for standard salutations on official correspondence. One of the items on the list was the proper method for addressing an abbot, a problem that we faced constantly, like at least once every millennium. One of my associates said that that was no problem. You simply yelled "Hey, A-b-b-b-b-o-o-o-t.")

Later in the year, when the chancery conducted a competition for the diocese's most popular teacher, Wintermeuler was at the ready with his own nomination papers. He prepared campaign posters that were actually quite clever. Because he was bald on top with dark sidewalls, his posters carried three headshot views: left profile, right profile, and bird's eye. Below the pictures was a bold-faced injunction to "Vote For This Man." The apparent willingness to make light of himself was a tactic designed to convince voters of his softer, gentler, less self-regarding side. Unfortunately, it was not enough to carry the day. Someone else won, and Wintermeuler returned to relative obscurity. He was eventually transferred from a chichi parish in Hyde Park (yes, Cincinnati had its own) to an impoverished church (St. Rose's) along Columbia Parkway, near the river. This was precisely the kind of hard duty which Wintermeuler needed.

Wintermeuler's History Club and its trips through the tri-state were rapidly eclipsed by the most profound force of our time: rock and roll music. We now know its roots. We didn't at the time. Rock and roll simply happened. One day there were Les Paul and Mary Ford, Kitty Kallen, Gogi Grant, and Vaughan Monroe; the next day there were Bill Haley, Duane Eddy, Chuck Berry, and Eddie Cochran. Schmaltz gave way to bop, though they coexisted uneasily for most of the decade. At the square dances at Fenwick Park, they had played slow dance songs like "Sentimental Journey" or worse. Many of the songs sung around the family piano were from the war, like the dance styles taught to us by Harris Rosedale in the St. Pete's bingo hall (group lessons at fifty cents apiece).

My uncle would walk into the room imitating Vaughan Monroe doing "Racing With the Moon," and the piano bench was stuffed with warmed-over Noel Coward and Cole Porter. Then came the beat, and the juxtaposition of old and new was indescribable. Think of Lawrence Welk at the Chateau Marmont or Keith Moon sitting in with the Modernaires.

Most of all, there was Elvis, and before Elvis the soldier, Elvis the actor, and Elvis the puffy icon, there was Elvis the singer, introduced to us on a series of immensely successful singles— "Heartbreak Hotel," "Hound Dog," and "Blue Suede Shoes," in particular. The streets and hallways and back seats of cars were suddenly filled with Sun and Decca records, and every party included a record player with the tubular 45 adapter in the center, stacked high with small disks. "Have you heard this yet?" was the standard question. Rock and roll had arrived, and its triumph was instantaneous.

There was something very populist about the 45. Album purchases were then seen as significant investments to be made only after considerable thought. The major record stores all included soundproof glass booths in which one could listen to a complete album before purchasing it. Given the fragility of vinyl and the threats posed by phonograph needle technology, this put the shop owner's inventory at some risk, a risk demanded by the market.

Wintermeuler had no patience with rock and roll and immediately counterattacked on several fronts, each tactic ultimately failing. First, he told us that rock and roll would never last and that we would remember our infatuation with it with both embarrassment and shame. He told us specifically that the type of song we would ultimately remember from our high school years would be a ballad like Pat Boone's "April Love." I pray that he is still alive and had the chance to see Pat Boone as faux biker punk, pierced, leathered, and tattooed, singing "Smoke on the Water." Wintermeuler did more than prophesy to us, however. He also mounted a major offensive to quash our taste for the devil's music.

The first phase was to pile on the homework on those nights when there were rock shows at Cincinnati Gardens. That failed quickly, since the poor students didn't care about their homework and the good students were able to finesse their way through the minor roadblock. Not that anyone spoke of "good" and "bad" students; each term would have been considered a slur. Instead, good students were labeled "smart," the point being that all of us shared common, antiacademic values and that those of us who somehow managed to receive good grades were doubtless victims of acts of God. Some girls were "good students," of course—another indication of the inscrutability of their nature and behavior.

Wintermeuler's second tactic was more subtle. He warned us that we should not go to rock concerts because it was "well known" that girls at rock concerts regularly became sexually aroused by the music. The point of that warning, presumably, was that we would feel extremely uncomfortable in the presence of sexually aroused members of the opposite sex. That argument actually gave certain people pause, though the reasons for their hesitation were never made explicit. An outraged religious sensibility? Male (pre-, pre-) performance anxiety? Fear of the unknown?

Regardless of Wintermeuler's threats, Bob and I soldiered on. The high point of our experience was actually seeing a live-and-in-person performance by the Crickets. Even today I can turn any eyes in the world green (particularly the eyes of rock musicians) by proudly telling them that I saw Charles Hardin "Buddy" Holl[e]y and the Crickets play.

Cincinnati Gardens

"Saw" is probably better than "heard," since the acoustics at Cincinnati Gardens were better for hockey and professional wrestling than for rock and roll. The sets were also very short. These were more rock shows than rock concerts. If memory serves, the Crickets played only three songs that evening: "Peggy Sue," "That'll Be the Day, " and "Maybe Baby."

Those who have seen Thomas Pynchon always seem to agree on a single, striking trait: his height. Buddy was tall as well, fronting the band in a trim and formal dark suit which matched the suits of the other Crickets and accentuated his long legs and the foot with which he kept time. He was far more gangly than Gary Busey and slightly stiffer and more businesslike in appearance. There was no rap with the audience, just a to-the-point, flawless performance.

Jerry Lee Lewis also played that night and brought the audience to their feet, despite the prohibitions of uniformed police who patrolled the venue. (Actual dancing in the aisles would have been met with instant arrest.) Jerry Lee was positioned at the edge of the stage on the audience's left (Buddy had been on the right), and the seat behind his piano kept him from standing or even moving comfortably. Eventually, he simply shoved it off the stage with the heel of his shoe and played standing. We were never sure if this had been carefully choreographed or was the result of simple frustration. It seemed authentic enough at the time, and when he did it, an audible gasp rose up from the audience.

The cops all tensed up, grabbing their Sam Browne belts like security blankets and saying more ejaculations than a convent full of Precious Blood nuns. They realized immediately the power of the music, and they knew it was uncontrollable and irreversible. One drum and one bass line and the hall was up for grabs. A single familiar line from a single song and the whole audience was moving together. Three, four thousand people? Nothing. Years later on a sloping lawn in southern Wisconsin, I heard the Eagles' last performance on their final tour before the *Hell Freezes Over* regrouping, heard them with twenty-two thousand other people, that is. By then the word had gotten around. Why didn't they invent this stuff sooner?

There were other acts, of course: Screaming Jay Hawkins screamed and Sam Cooke crooned. Danny and the Juniors sang their mandatory "At the Hop." In retrospect, I realize that these shows offered a spectrum of musical styles and traditions, all rooted in twelve-bar, black blues but finding their own ballad, rock, country, gospel, or rockabilly expressions. They also offered incredible value in those days when three or four lead acts (with an equal number of supporting groups) travelled together in hopes of increasing their growing audience.

The focus fell firmly on the music. There was little in the way of amplification. The sounds were raw. There were no flash pots, smoke, or other effects. We were years away from the flying pigs of Pink Floyd, the synchronized films of Supertramp, or the multi-storied sets and inflatable figures of the Rolling Stones.

We were also far closer to the source, the mix of black and white artists reminding us of the undergirding realities of the music. We learned that a spectrum of styles and forms could fit together naturally and effortlessly. The seventh chords which marked the blues simply worked their magic.

There is a wonderful story in Boswell of an acquaintance of Johnson's named William Barrowby. Dr. Barrowby loved pork and one day, when he was eating it, suddenly blurted out, "I wish I was a Jew." "Why so?" someone responded, since "the Jews are not allowed to eat your favourite meat." "Because," Barrowby answered, "I should then have the gust of eating it, with the pleasure of sinning."

That pretty well sums up our degree of gratitude to Father Wintermeuler, who added sexuality (perhaps with just an inch or two of racial edge) to our enjoyment of rock music. Guilty pleasures are always the best of all.

I had learned earlier that popular music could be used to deflate pretense and challenge authority, though the event was unrelated to rock and roll. The event was of a piece with the crazy quilt that was Cincinnati popular culture in the 1950s.

Each weekday at noon a local television personality named Ruth Lyons hosted a show entitled the *Fifty-Fifty Club*. The numbers referred to the size of the studio audience. The show began as the *Fifty Club* and extended its name when it doubled its audience. The show consisted of the conservative musings of Miss Lyons, with occasional interviews, musical interludes, tips on cooking, and extended commercials read or ad-libbed by the on-air talent.

Cincinnati was remarkable for the amount of local programming on its stations, particularly the NBC affiliate, Channel Five. Cleveland has been called the biggest small town in America, but the honors must surely be ceded to Cincinnati. Ruth Lyons was a central media figure in that 500,000-person village. Her early morning counterpart was a man named Paul Dixon, whose show was equally parochial and introspective, but slightly more naughty. One of Dixon's ongoing bits, for example, was a tracking shot of the legs of the women in the front row of his audience. He referred to this as his visit to "Kneesville."

Dixon had also been a member of the cast of the *Pantomime Hit Parade*, a CBS show, and one of his compatriots there—who later hosted the *Fifty-Fifty Club*—was a man named Bob Braun. Braun had outraged his Channel Nine boss by failing to mention the station when he was selected as a winner on the network show, *Arthur Godfrey's Talent Scouts*. Braun now does commercials in Los Angeles while his son Rob reads the evening news in Cincinnati.

The *Pantomime Hit Parade* was an odd show, in that it featured an extensive set of commercials for what was clearly a nonexistent product. This all-purpose substance was called All-Righty-Ro and the reasons for the simulated commercials which sung its considerable praises were never made clear. The star of the show was a woman named Dotty Mack (a much-shortened version of her long Italian surname), who later moved to New York and married the then-famous disk jockey, William B. Williams. The second female vocalist was a woman named Marian Spellman, who also eventually joined the *Fifty-Fifty Club*, where she was joined by a country vocalist from another local show—the *Midwestern Hayride*—Ruby Wright. Ruby's husband was a local band director, Barney Rapp, whose name is now attached to a travel agency.

The musical impresario of the *Fifty-Fifty Club* was a pianist named Cliff Lash. He was introduced to me as Clifford Lash at the zoo opera. We called it that since the performances were held at what was honorifically termed the Cincinnati Zoological Gardens. The theater—roofed to keep out the rain, but open at the sides to provide cross-ventilation—sat in the center of the zoo and invited the elephants, monkeys, big cats, and other neighbors to serve as active members of an unofficial chorus. I remember Mr. Lash well. He was meticulously dressed, polite, and somewhat shy. He looked as if he was late for a conservatory performance.

On the *Fifty-Fifty Club*, however, he was the smiling, outgoing showman, playing off of Ruth Lyons's persona as general empress and enlightened despot of WLW-T (the *T* distinguishing it from the affiliate's radio station). When she would press him to behave, he would suddenly launch into an up-tempo version of a conventional melody or play a kitsch classic like "Alley Cat." Ruth would then shake her head and say something like, "Isn't he naughty?" This was a distant cry from Jerry Lee Lewis kicking chairs off of stages and screaming "Great Balls of Fire," but to the women from the farm communities of the tri-state (the most vocal of which Ruth identified as "shouting Methodists") his behavior was daring beyond description.

It is one of the minor Cincinnati tragedies of my youth that when we received tickets to the *Fifty-Fifty Club* (the show was booked, literally, years in advance) Ruth Lyons was on vacation. The show was hosted by her sidekick Willie Thall, who eventually left the program and was forced to do commercials with one of the many Cincinnati merchants who had previously chosen to feature himself in lieu of professional actors. This was the owner of a discount house called Bargain City, who billed himself as the Bargain City Kid. The Kid dressed in a hillbilly/cowboy suit with a pistol belt and two miniature cap guns. His commercials with Willie consisted of a long plug that culminated in a duet in which the Kid mispronounced Willie's name:

". . . with the Bargain City Kid and Millie Small . . ."

"Thall."

"Doll."

"Thall."

"Moll."

And so on.

It was an ignominious close to what was widely perceived to be a distinguished career, even though the vanity commercial tradition was a serious one in the Queen City. The most distinguished representative of that cultural heritage was probably Kash D. Amburgy, who operated a furniture store in South Lebanon, a farm community between Cincinnati and Columbus. "Save Cash with

Kash" was his predictable slogan, but when Kash fell upon hard times and was desperately attempting to avoid bankruptcy, the slogan was altered to "Save Kash with Cash."

I never learned the reason for Willie's fall from grace. Perhaps he had attempted a level of obstreperousness with Miss Lyons that had exceeded the limits of her tolerance. Cliff Lash's musical improprieties were formulaic, even ritualistic, an expected part of the show. They were required elements in his job description. His putative disobedience was actually a form of obeisance. If Willie had attempted to challenge Miss Lyons, it had occurred behind the scenes, since he was always suitably adoring on camera.

Ruth Lyons was renowned in network circles for her ability to deliver a level of advertising revenue which was out of all proportion to the regional market. She was also the composer of a locally successful Christmas standby, "Let's Light the Christmas Tree," which was trotted out each holiday season. Her husband Herman, the subject of many on-air jibes, taught semantics at the University of Cincinnati; their adopted daughter Candy died, tragically, at an early age. For Cincinnatians of my generation (and the generation just before me), she was as important a part of local culture as Fountain Square, Empress Chili (later displaced by Skyline Chili and, to a degree, Gold Star Chili), Dave Frisch's Big Boy restaurants, and the Virginia Bakery.

The memories of the zoo opera (Jan Peerce singing Rigoletto, Risë Stevens doing Carmen, and Tomiko Kanazawa as Madame Butterfly) now jostle with thoughts of Cliff Lash sitting nearby, momentarily freed of the obligation to jerk Ruth Lyons's chain, the surrogate rebel for those who would not dare challenge the sovereign of the *Fifty-Fifty Club*. There were other rebels, however, and music was their frequent weapon. We sometimes forget that function enjoyed by rock and roll, a function that explains Pete Townsend's observation that the Beatles were pop singers, not rock and rollers.

Our singular act of high school rebellion—hanging the effigy of Father Matthew Forrest—was not accompanied with music. The silences spoke volumes, as a crowd of young men stood gaping at the sight before them. However, having learned the power of music in our studied efforts to annoy Father Wintermeuler, it should come as no surprise that an occasion presented itself, years later, for the full utilization of what Dryden called the power of music. Actually, this was a multimedia rebellion, but, on that, more later.

In this case, the unindicted conspirator was my old friend, Bob Kramer, the guy who had accompanied me to rock concerts at Cincinnati Gardens and risked the fires of hell by going with me to see *The Night Heaven Fell.* Bob had been through a lot in the intervening years, having joined and then left the priesthood. After taking his graduate work at Yale Divinity School, he was teaching at a local Catholic college when into his life walked a man from his past, a person he called the Infant of Prague.

The real Infant of Prague, of course, is Jesus, as imagined in a particular form of statuary—decidedly overdressed and notably regal for a small child. Infant of Prague statues were extremely popular in fifties churches. The richness of their regalia necessitated their being encased in protective glass to protect them from the sticky fingers of thieves or the soiled fingers of curious children. Kitsch versions featured plastic rather than gold crowns and sometimes had eyes that followed you around the room.

Bob's Infant, it turns out, was a vain priest named O'Connor, whose parents had saddled him with the given name of Victor. Though many suspected he liked the martial overtones of his first name, he chose to use his middle name, Kevin, instead.

V. Kevin O'Connor had been a prefect or assistant provincial or some such middle manager when Bob was in the novitiate, and he returned to haunt him later as the president of Bob's college. Kevin O'Connor had immediately and hungrily warmed to the role if not to the actual tasks which accompanied it, and, fixating on his own august presence, proceeded to destroy the institution and the morale of those who loved it.

"He contemplated himself as assiduously as Aristotle did the bust of Homer," Bob said, "always fussing with his cufflinks or checking to see if the collar of his pink Polo shirt was setting off

Grafton's Restaurant. The Three Boots Lounge is at the left front of the structure.

his neck and blond hair to full advantage. O'Connor wrecked everything his predecessor had worked to build and then proceeded to hire an assistant, a lawyer named Sullivan, to complete the task of institutional demolition. Sullivan played gray eminence (describing himself as 'the president's son-of-a-bitch') while O'Connor played . . . well . . . with himself. No one knew what to do. The board of directors sat like the See-, Hear-, and Speak-No-Evil monkeys, and every effort taken through proper channels to implore their intercession failed."

Bob was telling me about this at the Three Boots Lounge in Grafton's, an old Silverton restaurant that had been one of our favorites for many years. At first I thought he was depressed, as he threw back his martinis and worked his way into the story, but eventually I realized that he was warming to the task of telling me of Kevin O'Connor's downfall. He was getting into it, sip by sip, watching the suspense build as my questions multiplied.

"When it finally happened, it was nothing short of delightful," he said.

"What?" I asked.

"Relax," he said, "I'll tell you."

And he did. It was a masterpiece of planning. O'Connor had announced the date of his fall address to the faculty, an event for which the attendance had recently ebbed. The speech was advertised by flier, personal invitation, and spamming e-mail announcement. The words crawled across the electronic event board in the student union, the top and bottom of the college's home page, and even the scoreboard at the football stadium. Kevin was serious. So were Bob and his colleagues.

The speech was a sleeper from the first sentence, but the second (and final) act was Bob's. At the moment of what was intended to be the speech's peroration (when most in the audience were compulsively reading their programs in a desperate effort to stay awake), three events occurred which served to redirect their attentions.

First, the curtain behind Kevin O'Connor silently parted and the lights at the top of the stage came up, revealing a silent cement figure. It was a Cincinnati porch goose, the figure that had replaced the curb jockey and garden leprechaun in the city's material-culture kingdom. Such geese were regularly dressed in the fashion of the season, Thanksgiving pilgrim garb being a particular favorite. This one had a miniature roman collar and a child's-size, pink polo shirt. The collar was turned up. One overhead light gleamed across the goose's blond wig, which was even more noticeably false than Sam Donaldson's or Burt Reynolds's.

Then the goose pivoted on a circular trap door and faced a figure-length mirror which was drawn across the stage. Obviously pleased with the image he found therein, the barnyard Narcissus continued to turn in the direction of the mirror, lest he lose sight of his glorious visage and raiment.

Cincinnati porch goose

Finally, there was the music. It came booming over the PA system. One of Bob's coconspirators, a former Purcell classmate of ours named Chuck Hahnhorst, had edited a piece of tape and run it through the deck on a continuous loop. The song was "I Feel Pretty" from *West Side Story* and the key, repeating lyric was "A committeeee should be organized to honor meeeee." Bob hastened to add that it was not sung by Carol Lawrence, but rather by a local artist who had attained considerable notoriety in the city's counterculture: a 278-pound drag queen named Billy Breitenbach who sang a speaker-popping falsetto under the stage name of Eden Parks.

O'Connor stood there in shock, with a curdled-milk stare. The red flush along his throat was rising to the top of his head like a United Way thermometer. Just then, his toady, Michael Sullivan, rose up in a state of high dudgeon and marched toward the sound booth. By now what had started as lampoon turned quickly into opéra bouffe. The delicious part was that it had all been anticipated.

As Sullivan approached the booth, his way was blocked by a woman named Judy Nader, who was squatting in front of the door, appearing to look through the keyhole. The window blinds had been drawn and the door nailed shut with sixteen-penny finishing nails. The tape deck had been activated by a timer, set to go off exactly thirty minutes into O'Connor's speech. Attached to the same timer was a strobe light which was flashing wildly in time with the music. The light, like a small-scale electrical storm, could be seen through the keyhole and at the edge of the blinds.

Sullivan put his right hand on Judy's shoulder, pulled at her unceremoniously, and ordered her to get out of the way. She told him, sheepishly, that it was hard to see the people in the booth because of the strobe light. "Stand aside," he said, and wedged his head against the door jamb, pressing first his left and then his right eye against the keyhole. Thoughts of exquisite punishments for the culprits were doubtless racing through his head.

There was no one there, of course. After a period of at least two minutes, he stood up and stormed down the aisle toward O'Connor, who was still holding onto the lectern (his particular favorite, by the way, with his personally selected, carved mahogany seal) like a life preserver. When he looked down at Sullivan, his expression of vain hope went quickly south as his chin fell toward his chest.

Sullivan had taken the bait like a starving trout. His eyes were outlined by two large black circles of shiny soot. Comparisons were drawn with Smiley Burnette's horse, a reference that brought a rush of memories, though it was, regretfully, lost on the younger generations.

It was a moment worth years, even if it failed to bring O'Connor down as swiftly as Bob and his friends had hoped. The board dawdled, hemmed, and hawed, claimed that their president had several important initiatives to complete, and then quietly removed him a year and a half later. Sullivan, at least, failed to survive the week, though there were rumors of a platinum parachute, a necessity for O'Connor's wobbly conscience, since no one else in Cincinnati was likely to employ the "president's son-of-a-bitch."

"It was the music that did it," Bob said. "Every time he'd appear in public there would be a subterranean hum from the back of the crowd, the initial 'I Feel Pretty' melody reaching a crescendo with the '. . . honor meeeee' line. Each event was a small victory, but, taken together, they became decisive."

I opined that it was a pity that they hadn't thrown in some gangsta rap lyrics, since they would have been a little more earthy and to the point, but Bob persuaded me of the wisdom of sticking to our own generation's cultural devices. It was classic déjà vu all over again, with memories of Wintermeuler and Matthew Forrest and other acts of rebellion, small and large, crowding into our heads.

We finished our drinks, passed on dinner at Grafton's, and drove down to the White Castle in Norwood. They had moved it up the pike and shifted it to the west side of the street to make room for the crosstown connector between I-71 and I-75. We passed on the fries and cheeseburgers and other recent additions and went straight for the classic White Castles, starting with eight each and adding them in pairs, as needed.

The lights along the pike were bright, though there was an occasional bulb that needed to be replaced, and the Castle was doing more drive-through than walk-in business now. We sat in a corner, listening to the hum of conversation among the women working the grill, window, and counter. Except for the double-butter coffee cake from Virginia Bakery and the original Big Boy, this was nature's most nearly perfect food—patties in rows, crowded together, sizzling in onions, each covered by a bun to hold in the heat which passed through the holes in the patties (no need to turn them as they cooked that way). You could get them frozen, of course, and desperate people from out of town would have them

The remaining Norwood White Castle, remodeled and relocated

shipped, five or six dozen at a time, but there was never a substitute for the real thing—straight from the grill with a tiny pickle or two, nestled in groups of four on a small cardboard plate. We didn't confuse the taste with catsup or other additives but ate them as tradition dictated, four bites to the burger.

By then we didn't need to talk. We were where we wanted and needed to be: along a broad, winding road with buildings housing businesses that struggled to survive, buildings from the past that seemed not to have changed all that much, eating the food of our youth, looking out at the lights of the past which still managed to glimmer. Thinking about victories over petty tyrants. Thinking about the fact that we had survived; remembering. Home.

About the Author

Richard B. Schwartz is Dean of the College of Arts and Sciences at the University of Missouri-Columbia. He earned a BA in English from the University of Notre Dame, and an MA and PhD in English from the University of Illinois. He has published six books, including *Daily Life in Johnson's London, After the Death of Literature,* and *Frozen Stare,* a novel. He has also edited two collections and published many articles in journals such as *Studies in English Literature.*

About the Book

The Biggest City in America was designed and typeset by Kachergis Book Design of Pittsboro, North Carolina. The typeface, Adobe Caslon, was designed by Carol Twombly, and was based on specimen pages printed by William Caslon between 1734 and 1770. Caslon's types were based on seventeenth-century Dutch old style designs, which were then used extensively in England. Because of their incredible practicality, Caslon's designs met with instant success. Caslon's types became popular throughout Europe and the American colonies; printer Benjamin Franklin rarely used any other typeface. The first printings of the American Declaration of Independence and the Constitution were set in Caslon.

The Biggest City in America was printed on sixty-pound Glatfelter Natural Smooth and bound by Braun-Brumfield, Inc. of Ann Arbor, Michigan.

80025 75540